How to Take Over an American Public Company

by

Samuel H. Sloan

The Orsden Press
Berkeley, Tokyo

Published by
The Orsden Press
48 Shattuck Square, Suite 666
Berkeley, CA 94704-1140
U.S.A.

ISBN 1-881373-01-0

The Japanese translation may be ordered from:

The Orsden Press
CPO Box 2126
Tokyo, Japan

First Printing April 1992
Printed in Japan

Table of Contents

Acknowledgments

I need to thank many people for assistance in giving me the knowledge which enabled me to write this book.

At the top of the list goes Al Miller, the President of Shareholder Communications Corporation of 40 Exchange Place in New York City. Al gave me a job back in 1976 writing tender offer materials, letters of transmittal, prospectuses and related documents, at a time when everybody else on Wall Street was afraid to associate with me because I was public enemy number one on the official list of the S.E.C., because I was trying to put them out of business. Al was the only one who still believed in me back then.

Because of the experience working for Al over the next five years, I learned most of what I know about the tender-offer game. I hope that I have not given away too many of his secrets in this book.

As far as the bad guys at the S.E.C. were concerned, I finally beat them 9–0 in the United States Supreme Court, after I argued my own appeal orally before the full panel. You can look it up. **S.E.C. v. Samuel H. Sloan**, 436 U.S. 103 (1978).

I must thank Mike Goodall and Luis Busquets. Both of them are chess players. I have known them for 30 years and 22 years respectively. They provided me with backup and support during a recent tender offer I conducted, which brought me up to date on the latest developments in the law. They were the only ones who stood behind me and who believed that I could do it.

I also need to thank a certain unscrupulous and entirely crooked attorney from the opposing side, who taught me a few dirty tricks which I never otherwise would have dreamed to be possible.

I need to thank Gregg W. Corso of the United States Securities and Exchange Commission Office of Tender Offers for his lengthy lectures and tutoring. Gregg spent many hours explaining the law to me in simple terms which even I could understand, and issued various homework assignments, not to mention ultimatums, thereby giving the information I needed to write this book.

Lastly, I must mention my father, Leroy B. Sloan, formerly a lawyer and auditor with the Internal Revenue Service. My father used to talk to me daily about the stock market, starting from the time when I was about six years old. His father, in turn, had been a heavy player of the stock market until he got wiped out in the 1929 crash. I realized just before my father died in 1986 that it was his daily discussions with me from an early age about the workings of the stock market which imparted to me his deep level of understanding and provided me with a way to make a living for a lifetime.

About the Author

Samuel H. Sloan was born in Richmond, Virginia in 1944. He bought his first share of stock on his own initiative with his own money in 1956 when he was eleven years old. From that age forward, he was a regular reader of stock market information services and reports. He was a winner in the Virginia Science Talent Search, and made an 800 in his mathematics college boards. He majored in mathematics at the University of California at Berkeley, where he was actively involved in the Free Speech Movement and was the president of a well-known on-campus student organization. He also established a master rating at chess.

In 1968, he got a job working in the over-the-counter trading department of Hayden-Stone, Inc. in New York City. He got that job primarily because they mistakenly believed that he was the son of a famous man, also named Samuel Sloan, who was a member of the New York Stock Exchange.

However, before long, he became more famous than his namesake. He learned everything about the over-the-counter trading market and was known for taking the pink sheets home with him at night and studying them. By 1970, he has established his own firm, Samuel H. Sloan & Co., which, over a period of the next five years, made a market in thousands of over-the- counter stocks and bonds.

During that five years, in 1971, he became a primary target of the Securities and Exchange Commission under Chairman William Casey. It is not clear why the S.E.C. devoted so much attention to him, except that they seemed to express the belief that he must be the front man for somebody else, because they considered it impossible for a man so young to be so actively involved in the stock market, doing all the things that he was doing.

The S.E.C.'s curiosity about Sloan clashed with Sloan's natural tendency to rebel against governmental authority acquired through active involvement in the Free Speech Movement. This led to a series of lawsuits, with the S.E.C. suing Sloan and Sloan suing the S.E.C. Eventually, the matter reached the United States Supreme Court in 1978. Sloan won 9-0, after arguing his appeal pro se.

However, the numerous unfair and prejudicial press releases issued by the S.E.C. against Sloan and the resulting unwanted publicity in the *Wall Street Journal* made it difficult for him to work in the securities industry. He therefore went to Kabul, Afghanistan, where he nearly lost his life in the 1978 communist take-over. After spending three months as a political prisoner of the new communist government, he went from there to Chitral, Pakistan, where he became fluent in the local language, which is Khowar, and eventually wrote the *Khowar-English Dictionary* of that previously almost completely unrecorded language. He later traveled to 74 countries of the world, lived in El Salvador, Japan, and Sri Lanka and finally settled in the United Arab Emirates. He returned to America in November, 1990, during the Gulf War.

Sloan is also an active writer in the field of chess. He knows personally almost all of the world's leading chess grandmasters, and is friends with many of the world's leading chess personalities, including Bobby Fischer, the Polgar sisters and Xie Jun, the new World's Woman Chess Champion. He was the chess columnist for the *Gulf News* in the United Arab Emirates.

In addition, Sloan is a three-dan player of Japanese Chess (shogi) and holds a third-grade certificate in Chinese chess (xiangqi). He is considered one of the leading western players in the world in both of these games. In 1989, he finished second in Singapore in the World Championship for non-Chinese of Chinese chess. He is also considered to be the strongest non-Thai player in the world of the game of Thai chess. Sloan is the author of a book: *Chinese Chess for Beginners.*

Sloan has seven children, whose names are Peter, Mary, Shamema, Michael, Jessica, George and Anusha.

Introduction

Anyone who regularly reads the financial section of any American newspaper has come across the term 'Corporate Raid'. This term evokes the vision of a commando operation, with paratroopers jumping in and attacking an unsuspecting target.

It can, in reality, be a little bit like that.

This is a 'How to do It' book. It is intended to teach something which few people know anything about, which is how to conduct a corporate raid. There are almost no books on this subject, not even in the major law libraries in America. Anyone who has this knowledge finds it too valuable to write about and to reveal to others. Indeed, one reason for not publishing this book in America is to keep this knowledge out of the hands of the people who might best be able to use it.

Right now, Japan needs this knowledge. Perhaps also America needs to let Japan know how to do these things. America is on the skids. The American economy is bad, and is going to get worse. Why is that? The reason is that America does not know how to adapt to a changing world. America is used to being the world's leading economy. America has the idea that everybody has to come to America and that America does not need to go anywhere else. America does not understand that something fundamental has changed in the world's economy. The world will never be again like it was before.

Right now, America seems to be thinking that if it can just get rid of George Bush and get somebody else, things will get better. 'Prosperity is just around the corner', is what America is saying. America does not understand: 'Those days are finished. It is all gone. From now on, America will have to compete in the world's economy. America can no longer make a profit just by selling to its own market.'

Americans do not have the concept of saving money. They spend what they get, as soon as they get it. More than that, they go to the bank and borrow against their future earnings, and spend that money quickly too.

Right now, nobody in America has money. They have already spent it all. There is no money in America for capital investment or for capital improvements. Therefore, America is looking around and trying to find somebody else who has money.

Japan, of course, has money. Why is that? Because the Japanese people save their money. They put it in the bank. They don't spend it all right away. This causes a big complaint from America. This is called 'Japan bashing'. 'Why don't the Japanese spend their money like Americans do,' they say. 'This is not fair. They should all pull their money out of the savings banks, and use it to buy a new Cadillac, with a steering wheel on the left-hand side.'

However, nobody in Japan really needs a new Cadillac. Nobody in America seems to understand that. America needs money, and needs it quickly. Everything in America is for sale right now. There is nothing in America that cannot be bought. Why anybody would want to buy anything in America is another question. We just assume that there are still things in America worth buying. The question is: 'How to do it'. America wants to sell everything, and right now only

Japan has the money to buy it all.

This book is, therefore, intended for enterprising Japanese executives who want to enlist America as a suitable slave-colony of Japan. However, the average Japanese businessman (or even the average American businessman, for that matter) will not know much about American securities regulations. Hence, the need for this book.

Chapter One

Why Buy America?

America is like the proverbial ostrich with its head in the sand. Nobody in America seems to understand that there has just been a fundamental change in the world. Remember the Soviet Union? It doesn't exist any more! What does this mean? What this means is that the old order of things has now changed.

A long, long time ago, way back in 1991 or thereabouts, there used to be two competing powers in the world: America and the Soviet Union. Everybody had to join one side or the other. There was really no third choice. Anybody who tried to stay in the middle and play against both sides, was playing a dangerous game. The Prime Minister of Afghanistan did that. Look at what happened to him.

The smart side bet on America. Those who did so got rich. Those who bet on the Soviet Union got poor.

Throughout history, the countries who were poor always attacked the countries who were rich. This historical fact made everybody who lived in a rich country convinced that the Soviet Union or another country allied with the Soviet Union was going to attack. Perhaps the country most convinced of this was West Germany. The Soviet Union was always 'saber rattling' against West Germany. They said that the formation of the West German state was 'illegal' because it violated the agreements made by the four great powers to divide Germany into four parts after the war. This kind of talk made West Germany very nervous. Any German who had money wanted to use it to buy a house or a farm in America. They all wanted a place to which to run, as soon as the East Germans attacked.

Today, this sounds ridiculous. However, the fact is that just a few years ago, almost everybody in West Germany was convinced that a Soviet Union attack was only a few days away.

What is the German businessman with his house and farm in America doing right now? Everybody knows the answer. He is trying to sell it. He is selling it because he wants to use the money to buy a factory in what used to be East Germany. He is no longer afraid of a Soviet attack. The Soviet Union doesn't exist any more. The Russians are just begging for food to give themselves something to eat. They are in no position to attack anybody.

What does this all mean? This means that all of the smart money, amounting to billions of dollars, is right now being pulled out of America by the Germans and invested in Latvia. In Latvia? Yes, right now, Latvia is where the action is. Nobody in Germany is going to invest in America, when much better investments are available in Latvia. Latvia has a stable, highly educated work force. Latvia is cheap. Latvia is only a few hundred miles away from the major markets in Germany. Latvia has beautiful women, not a minor consideration for the average German businessman looking for a place to spend his money.

America has not even thought about this. 'Why is nobody knocking at my door any more?', America is asking. 'Ah yes, it must be because of that terrible George Bush. Because of him, nobody wants to buy our products any more,' America is saying. America is just not capable of understanding that all of the smart money is going into Latvia and the other countries of Eastern Europe right now.

'Okay, you've convinced me,' says the reader. 'I'm going to book the first flight to Riga, Latvia right now. Incidentally, wasn't this supposed to be a book about taking over American companies.'

Actually, while it is true that much of the smart money in what used to be West Germany is going into Latvia right now, America is still a more suitable place for investment from the point of view of Japan. Japan has a tremendous amount of excess capital. America has no money, and everything is for sale.

There is a problem with money. You have to use it or lose it. You cannot simply stuff money into a mattress. Money has to be moved. It has to keep moving all the time. Putting money into a bank account does not make it stand still. When you put your money into a bank, the bank loans it to somebody else, who uses it to buy something else. There is no such thing as 'safe money'.

Business is the same way. You have a product. It sold well last year. However, it will not sell well this year. It will not sell at all next year. Somebody else will make something better. You have to work all the time. You always have to be working to make your product better, and, at the same time, you always have to be looking for new products to sell. The same old product that was selling well before, just isn't good enough to sell any more.

Japan understands this point. American management does not. America just wants to sit on its traditional advantage. America is stagnant. America does not understand that it is standing still, while the rest of the world is moving.

What America needs right now is to be taken over by the Japanese. Top level management in America does not exist any more. All of the old line managers, the men who made America great, the men who knew the value of profit, the men who understood the importance of the bottom line, those men are all dead now, or are sitting in old-age nursing homes. American management is now a bunch of Dan Quayles. 'Mr. Blow Dried' is the typical corporate manager. America is a nation of 'whiz kids'; children who know how to push paper, but who do not know or even care about how to make a product that the public will want to buy.

Remember Donald Trump? Nobody heard of him a few years ago and, soon, nobody will hear of him again, except for possibly the latest news about his mistress or his latest bankruptcy proceedings. They are all like that. They rise quickly and they fall just as fast. Anybody who has spent any length of time in the stock market has seen dozens of these flashy names come and go. How many people still remember Bernie Cornfield? How many people still remember James Ling? How many people still remember Tino D'Angelis? All of them were more famous than Donald Trump. All of them are still alive today, happy to have their names finally out of the daily news. There have been many more like them. They obey the law of gravity: What goes up, must come down. Like a comet in the sky, they appear and disappear just as quickly.

Why is that? The reason is because they never ever made a real profit on anything that they did. Donald Trump never made a nickel as the result of any general business operation. He, and the others, just got to the top by reading the rules and filing the forms with the S.E.C. Profit in the business was the last thing on their minds. You don't need a profit if you are always getting in new money all the time.

Chapter Two

Getting Started

The purpose of this book is to explain how to take over American public companies. The first point to be understood is that America has private companies and public companies. Private companies are often family or individually owned. Public companies are traded in the stock market. There are more than 50,000 public companies. There are only a few exceptions to the general rule that all of the really major American companies are public. To acquire a private company, one needs to negotiate a deal with the owner, or owners, of that company. However, to purchase a public company, one needs to only buy a majority of the outstanding shares in the open stock market. Anybody with a majority of the shares of a public company gets to throw out the old management and replace it with his own new management. Anybody can buy any American public company; all he needs is to have the money and the know-how to do it.

At this point, it is time for a little basic instruction. An explanation is needed of what the stock market is and how it works. This might seem to be too elementary for many readers. However, in order for a baby to walk, he must first learn how to crawl. Equally, in order to conduct a corporate raid on the stock market, one needs first to understand exactly how the stock market works.

After I introduce myself as a stock market person, the

question which I am asked most often goes something like this: 'What is the stock market? I have heard, of course, about buying and selling shares. Every day in the news, I hear about the Dow Jones Industrial Average going up or down. But I still don't understand it. If I buy a stock, what am I buying? Is it like buying a cow in the stock yards? What do I get for my money? Please explain this to me.'

The fact is that there are many people, even among those who are working directly in the stock market, who do not know exactly what the stock market is. This may seem surprising.

Those who work directly in the stock market in America often think of it as a building located near the corner of Broad and Wall Streets in the financial district of New York City. Most of them, even among those who work there, do not really understand much about what goes on inside of that building or what the need or the purpose of it is.

In more distant locations, most people do not think of the stock market as being located at a particular place. To them, it is even more mysterious.

Actually, the stock market is not really so difficult to understand. The reason that most people do not understand it is that they do not understand the underlying concept.

I will try to explain the concept of the stock market in simple and general terms. I will try to avoid technical matters. What I want to explain is the idea of the stock market, without getting bogged down in details.

This is not an easy task. It involves taking a complex and difficult subject and reducing it to simple terms. To make matters worse, this is a subject which most people know at least a little bit about. Whenever I try to say anything about the stock market, there is always somebody who interrupts and says: 'That is not true. It isn't like that at all. Rather, it is the other way.' And with that, he or she proceeds to go off into a completely different direction.

I am not trying to say that whatever this other person has to say is wrong and that what I have to say is right. I am also not trying to imply that I know more about it than that other person does. Probably, that other person knows more than I do. What I am trying to do is something different. I am trying to reduce the ideas involved in the stock market to simple terms which even a beginner can understand.

In the course of doing this, this book will be filled with statements with which almost nobody will completely agree. Almost everybody will claim that I am wrong and that I simply don't know what I am talking about. Proof will be offered to show that what I say is complete nonsense.

The reason that I know in advance that all this will happen is that every time I try to explain the stock market to a group of people, there is always someone who interrupts and disagrees with what I am saying. Usually, in the end, I just have to tell that person to shut up and wait until I am finished. This solution is not really satisfactory.

What I am trying to do right now is to explain the stock market in just a few pages, using small words printed with big letters which even a child can understand. Obviously, there are going to be problems with doing this. Even a book of one thousand pages would not be adequate to begin to explain the stock market. How do I propose to do it in just a few pages?

Actually, this problem is not quite so impossible as it might at first seem. The beauty of the stock market is that it involves a universally recognized system of doing business. More importantly, it is a system on which everybody who works within the system agrees. Even more than that, it is a tried, tested and proven system.

A system which was too complicated to be understood by the average person would be unworkable and would quickly collapse. In spite of the dire predictions to the contrary, the stock market has never collapsed. (See what I mean. Already there are the hands of people going up from those eager to tell me that the stock market collapsed in 1929, and then collapsed again in 1987, and for that matter collapsed on many other less well known occasions along the way. However, what I mean to say is that in spite of all of these temporary ups and downs, the stock market is still there, working, functioning and operating every day, after the passage of hundreds of years, while even great empires emerged, rose, fell, and vanished from existence. Just as the stock market was here more than two hundred years ago, there is every reason to believe that it will still be here more than two hundred years from now. About what other institution can such a statement be made?)

Actually, there is one point to bear in mind. The stock market is a system within which tens of thousands of people live and work. Everybody within the system understands at least how his or her small part of the system works. For example, a clerk who works in the stock loan department of a major stock brokerage firm will be likely to know everything there is to know about stock loan. On the other hand, he might not know much about margin. In fact, unless he has a friend working in the margin department or has once worked there himself, he will probably not know even what the margin department of a stock brokerage firm is, much less what it does. In fact, he will very possibly not really understand what a share of stock really is. In spite of all this, he might be an excellent stock loan clerk, a master of his chosen profession. Even if he had a full understanding of the overall stock market system, it would not help him much or enable him to do his job any better.

Since the stock market embodies a system which is universally agreed upon and accepted, it follows logically that it must be possible to explain it in simple terms to be understood by the average person.

In reality, the stock market is an idea. It is not really a place any more. The New York Stock Exchange is older than the United States of America. Tradition has it that the New York Stock Exchange was founded as a meeting place under a buttonwood tree more than 200 years ago. It was a private club for doing business. Membership was by invitation only. All members were required to charge fixed commissions to all non-members, but were not allowed to charge a commission to each other. Any member who violated these rules got expelled from the club. Only dues paying members of the club were allowed to meet and do business under the buttonwood tree. Eventually, the members of the club became so successful and so prosperous that they were able to buy their own building and move indoors.

At one time, not so very many years ago, you could say that the New York Stock Exchange was in a building, whereas the less prosperous American Stock Exchange was out on the street corner nearby. At that time, the American Stock Exchange was known as the 'Curb Exchange', because it was literally located out on the curb of a public street. In the winter, they used to stand out on the street in their snowboots, signaling by hand to brokers leaning out of the windows many floors above. They finally went indoors only in 1953. However, they still use the same system of hand signals.

Nowadays, with worldwide telecommunications, it is no longer meaningful to describe the stock market as being located at one particular place. The stock market is now more of a world-wide computer network.

This is why I keep referring to the 'idea' or the 'concept' of the stock market. The stock market is something which cannot be seen. It has to be visualized or imagined.

Here is the way in which I try to explain the stock market which has proven to be the most successful:

Let us start with any basic business. For example, let us say we want to open a bakery shop which makes and sells cakes and cookies. In order to start this bakery, first we rent a shop. Then we buy an oven. Next, we hire a baker. Then, we buy flour and other ingredients. We buy cooking oil. We put the baker to work baking cookies. We hire a sales person to deal with the customers. After all this, we are ready to start the business.

However, in order to do all this, we have had to spend money. We have spent many thousands of dollars, pounds, rubles or whatever. Up until now, we have not had one penny of income. In short, we have risked a lot of money, with no guarantee or assurance of return.

Still, we are not seriously worried. We know that as long as we have a qualified baker and that our prices are reasonable, somebody will buy our cookies. The proof of this is that on the next street corner, a successful bakery shop has been in operation for many years. Of course, our business may succeed or it may fail. It may have a profit or it may have a loss. That is a different subject. The point is that we are doing a well established and well known type of business which has already been done successfully many times in the past. We have enough money to start this new business on our own. Any profits which we make will belong entirely to us. Any losses we suffer we will be prepared to bear ourself.

Now, let us imagine that we are not satisfied to spend our lives running a small bakery shop. What we want to do instead is that we want to build an automobile factory. However, this particular factory will not build normal automobiles. Our automobiles will run 200 miles on one gallon of gas, or else will use free solar energy, or will sail in the ocean, or will fly into outer space, or will be powered by a perpetual motion machine of a new design and type. All this can be done for the price of a mere 800 billion dollars to build the first prototype and, after that, to build the factory to make them.

Of course, there is only one problem with this, which is that no one person has 800 billion dollars to spend to build this wonderful and much needed factory. That is where the stock market comes in.

Actually, if you take any decent-sized company which is listed on the New York Stock Exchange, you will see that even the richest person in the world does not have enough money to buy it all, without borrowing heavily from banks and other sources. Even Shaikh Zayid bin Sultan Al Nahyan, the Ruler of Abu Dhabi, does not have so much money. Nobody has so much money, or would be willing to spend or risk that much money even if he had it. Therefore, the stock market has been created to fulfill this basic need.

Let us take, for example, the General Motors Corporation. I am using this as an example only because the name of this corporation is well known. Many other corporations provide equally valid examples.

There was once more than one hundred companies making cars in America. The top corporate 'blue chip' was called Auburn Motors. Auburn Motors was considered a 'safe' investment. We all now know how safe it was. Auburn Motors does not exist any more.

Today, there are only three car makers in America. What this means is that of the more than 100 original car makers, 97 lost money and went out of business. Only three survived. Nevertheless, the car business became the biggest business in America.

Why is that? Isn't it amazing that almost everybody in the biggest business in America lost money and that only a few made a profit?

A significant fact is that even the most successful companies in America make only a few percentage points profit on their capital investments. More than that, those which do make a profit are required to pay taxes. After taxes, they are under a certain obligation to pay a dividend to their investors.

After these and other payments, it has been estimated that the invested capital in any listed corporation, regardless of how successful, produces less than two percent of profits which are used for capital growth and expansion. At a rate of two percent real growth, it would take thirty-five years for any company, regardless of how successful, to double in size.

Returning again to General Motors, think about the fact that cars did not even appear on the roads in significant numbers until 1910 or thereabouts. Nevertheless, by 1937, General Motors was one of the largest corporations in the entire world. Did General Motors get that big that fast solely by plowing profits back into capital improvements? No, that would have been impossible. Rather, it got big quickly by raising money through the sale of shares in the stock market. The public investors could see that General Motors had the potential to grow quickly, and so were willing to invest their money. Because of this, General Motors leaped ahead of Ford Motors, which originally had been the leader in the car production field. Ford Motors remained a family owned business until it finally saw the light and went public in 1956. For that reason, Ford Motors remains second to General Motors to this day.

The point is that the stock market provides a mechanism which enables companies to raise money for capital expansion and improvement, money which could not be obtained in any other way. The money raised through the stock market enables companies to grow quickly. The investors who buy shares of stock become part owners in the company, and they can buy or sell their shares at any time.

Imagine, for example, that a new corporation is formed to power cars with solar energy. One million shares are issued. Each of these one million shares is sold to investors for $10 per share. As a result, the company starts its life with

$10,000,000. Every year, there is a corporate election. The owner of each share has one vote. A person who owns 1000 shares has 1000 votes. There are seven directors. Any person can run for election as a director. Whoever gets the most votes wins. Those who win election as directors get to run the company. At the same time, anybody who owns shares can sell them in the stock market. If the company is successful and makes a profit, eventually it will pay dividends to the shareholders.

Chapter Three

How to Form a U. S. Corporation

In order to be traded in the stock market, one needs to form a corporation. Why is that? The reason is that the stock market is a place where shares of publicly held corporations are traded. Partnerships and individuals are not traded in the stock market. Only shares of corporations are traded there.

When one company decides to take over another company, the acquiring company often finds it convenient to form a fresh corporation which does nothing else buy the company being taken over.

A corporation contains permanent capital. This is a point of utmost importance. Let us say that a private individual starts a business. Over the course of many years, he makes a lot of money. He expands and builds his business up. He brings in his sons, his daughters, and his grandchildren. The entire family gets rich. This becomes a big business. Annual sales exceed $100,000,000 dollars. The product is popular. Everybody wants to buy it. It seems like this can go on forever.

Then what happens? What happens is that the old man dies. The sons and the daughters don't want the business any more. They want their money, and they want it now, right away. They were just hanging around to keep the old man happy and to make sure that they got their fair share when he died. They start fighting among each other over the money. The business is so big that none of them can afford to buy it. Soon, they start to liquidate. Everything is sold at a fraction of the real value. All the machinery and equipment is disposed of at public auction. The business ceases to exist.

This happens all the time. Eventually, almost every family owned business winds up like this. This is the reason that, in America, almost every big business is now owned by a corporation.

What the old man should have done to perpetuate his name for all eternity was to form a corporation. He should have put all of his assets into the corporation and then issued shares of stock to himself. When his sons grew up, he could have given them some of that stock. When he died, they would have sold that stock in the stock market to somebody interested in running the business. They would have gotten their money and the business would have gone on. A corporation never really dies. Only the ownership of the shares changes hands.

A corporation is an individual which exists only on paper. This is a concept which is difficult to understand. A corporation is a creature created on paper by the state. A corporate person can do almost anything in business that a real person can do. A corporation can buy, sell, lend and lease. The real persons who work for the corporation are its agents. However, under the law, a corporation is regarded as a person. A corporation can even be convicted of a crime. It would be difficult to put a corporation in jail, but a corporation can be forced to pay a fine.

In America, corporations are registered by states. Every corporation in America has a state of incorporation. A California corporation is a different sort of animal which exists under different laws from a Delaware Corporation. However, in Japan and in most other countries of the world, this federal system of government does not exist. No matter where in the country the corporation is formed, the rules for that corporation are the same.

In America, most of the major corporations are formed in the State of Delaware. The reasons for this are historical. Delaware is a small state which feels a need to attract businesses. For this reason, it has encouraged business to come there from other states. The corporate tax and fees in Delaware are low. A corporation with millions of shares outstanding and millions of dollars in profits every year will still have to pay a low annual fee in Delaware.

This is important. A corporation is an artificial person and can only exist by permission of the state. Once that state withdraws its permission, the corporation ceases to exist.

A corporation must pay its corporate tax. Unlike a natural person, it cannot become a tax fugitive and run away and hide from the law in another jurisdiction. If a corporation fails to pay its state corporate tax, its charter can be revoked by the state and it could cease to exist.

Delaware, once a poor state, has gotten rich because of its ability to attract corporations to come there. The vast majority of all corporations with stock traded on the New York Stock Exchange were formed in Delaware. For this reason, most of the major cases involving corporate law are heard and decided in the Delaware Chancery Court. You, too, will be there soon, before this book is over.

In recent years, some other states have liberalized their

laws to attract business. Nevada has established lower fees than Delaware. Budget minded corporate executives are starting to show a preference for incorporation in the State of Nevada. However, Nevada has an image problem. Nevada is a state associated with sleazy, fly-by-night corporations which run away and disappear overnight. Traditionally, nobody has wanted to buy stock in a company incorporated in Nevada.

Nevada has, to some extent, solved its image problem. In fact, recent surveys have shown that Nevada is the fastest growing state in the United States, with the lowest level of unemployment. At the same time, Delaware has raised its fees. Delaware is no longer a 'cheap' state in which to incorporate.

As a result, a lot of smart businessmen who know exactly what they are doing, are starting to incorporate in Nevada. There are other small states who are also trying to cash in on this bonanza by changing their corporate rules and lowering their fees. Wyoming is possibly a state to consider when forming a new corporation. This is a constantly changing subject, about which one needs to know the latest information.

However, in order to be on the safe side, it is probably best to incorporate in Delaware. Delaware is still the state of choice for many knowledgeable executives. The extra fees there are almost inconsequential. Most of the famous names among corporations are incorporated in Delaware.

To incorporate in Delaware is a simple process. To make it even simpler, there are several registered companies who will do all of the paper work for this. The best, or at least the best known, of these is The Company Corporation in Wilmington,

Delaware. Everybody knows them. Their address is Three Christina Center, 201 North Walnut St., Wilmington, Delaware 19801, tel. (302) 575-0440, FAX (302) 575-1346. Just call them up and ask for Allison Maxwell. Tell her the name of the corporation that you want to form. She will reserve that name for you with the State of Delaware for 30 days. Nobody else can form a corporation under that name during that period. The Company Corporation will send you the forms. Fill them out and mail them back, along with your fee. They will offer you various services, and each one has a fee. However, this will not be expensive. Their basic fee to form a corporation is $119. Pay that fee, and you will be in business. All of their fees for all of their services will cost not more than $200, at least at the initial stages. Remember that they do a hundred of these every day.

An important service which they will perform for you is that they will act as your 'registered agent'. In most states, you must maintain an office within that state in order to form a corporation there. Delaware does not have that rule, which is a good reason for wanting to form a corporation in Delaware if your actual office is in Japan or in some other country. However, even in Delaware, you must have a registered agent there for service of process. The Company Corporation will perform that service for you, provided that you pay their low annual fee.

This book is not, by the way, intended to be an advertisement for The Company Corporation. There are no doubt many other agents who will perform the same services for you cheaper and better. However, The Company Corporation is the 'Tiffany' of its field. Everybody else uses them, so you might as well use them too.

The Company Corporation will also form corporations for you in any other state of the United States, including Nevada, so they can be used for that purpose as well.

Once you have your corporation, you will need to have a 'corporate kit'. A corporate kit contains a minute book and your corporate seal, plus shares of stock, among the other things which your corporation will need. This you can also order from The Company Corporation, but another company located on Canal Street near Varick Street in New York City is better for that. They will charge you about $100 for everything you need. For a slightly higher fee, your new corporate minute book will come in original leather, if you are interested in such things.

When you form your corporation, you will need to decide on certain things. Most importantly, you will need to decide on a name, a par value and the number of shares of stock to be authorized.

These are important decisions to make, because each state will tax you differently on the basis of this. In some respects, incorporating in Delaware can be a trap. Their fees are lower at the beginning, but get higher later on. Since this changes from year to year, this book will not attempt to deal with that subject.

Generally, in Delaware, the tax is calculated by multiplying the number of shares times the 'par value' per share. The term 'par value' once meant the amount at which the shares were originally sold. Nowadays, it is more of a bookkeeping entry. Again, this varies from state to state. In Delaware or in Nevada, you might find it preferable to have a corporation with 10,000,000 shares of stock originally authorized, at a par value of $0.0001 per share. (That is: one-one hundredth of one cent per share). This means that all the shares of stock combined have a par value of a total of $1,000. You pay taxes only on that.

In fact, Nevada corporations, rather than Delaware corporations, tend to be like that. However, you would not want to form a corporation in Virginia like that. In Virginia, you pay an annual tax of $25 for each 25,000 shares of stock authorized. In other states, the method of calculation is different. In those states, it might be best to have stock with no par value. This would be disastrous for tax purposes in Delaware, however. You would be taxed at the maximum rate.

Again, you need to check the tax laws of the state before forming a corporation within that state. A call to The Company Corporation in Wilmington, Delaware will provide you with that information.

You will also need a corporate name. In America, names often are something like 'AAA Trucking Company, Inc.' The reason for this is that they want to be first in the yellow pages of the telephone book. In just about every telephone book in America, you will find an AAA Trucking Company listed, and just above that, an AAAA Trucking Company. Somewhat lower in the telephone book, there will be an 'Acme Trucking Company'. This is the reason that 'Acme' is such a popular name among companies in America. It comes at an early point in the alphabet.

If you don't care about being first in the yellow pages of the telephone book, just about any name will do, as long as somebody else in the state where you are incorporating does not already have that name.

Another way to form a corporation is to go to an American lawyer. He will call The Company Corporation and do all the things that you would have done. He will charge you a fee of about $1,000 for this service, plus all the fees which The Company Corporation is charging him for all of these same services.

The corporation is formed by an 'incorporator'. Once the corporation is formed, the incorporator appoints the initial directors. From that point on, these directors conduct the business of the corporation. They sell shares, usually at par value, to persons who become the initial stockholders in the corporation. Later on, the stockholders can hold elections, vote those directors out, and elect new directors. From that point on, the company is owned by the stockholders, but run by the directors, who, in turn, appoint the president, secretary, treasurer and other corporate officers.

Delaware is the preferred state for those corporations which are involved in stock market activities. However, if the corporation you want to form will never be involved in the stock market, there are many other states which are cheaper and better than Delaware.

One of the first things which will happen after you have incorporated in Delaware is that you will receive a tax bill from the State of Delaware for something like $147,583.79. Naturally, you may find this discouraging. You thought that this all was going to cost you less than $200. However, not to worry. This is the maximum tax payable, as calculated by the state. You have to get information on the Delaware corporate taxes and recalculate the tax yourself. In all likelihood, the initial tax will be less than $200 per year.

After the corporation has been formed, it will need an Internal Revenue Service tax identification number. The Internal Revenue Service has a special telephone number in Washington, D.C. that you can call to get this tax ID number assigned to your corporation. Before that, you have to obtain the required forms from the Internal Revenue Service. These will be available at the local IRS office in any city in America. They might also be available in a local U.S. Embassy. Fill in the forms, call the IRS, and read the information on the forms, line by line, over the telephone. You will have to wait about a half hour on the telephone, but the tax identification number will be assigned to your corporation on the same day. However, if you want to save on your telephone bill, you can send the forms in the mail and hope to get an answer from the IRS within two or three weeks.

Once you have your tax identification number, you will be able to open a bank account and conduct the business of the corporation.

Chapter Four

How Shares Come to be Traded in the Stock Market

Once a corporation has been formed, it needs money to operate. Remember that a corporation is an artificial person. It can do anything in business that a natural person can do. When a corporation is formed, it has a certain number of shares which are authorized. However, these shares have not, as yet, been issued. The first shares are usually issued to the founders of the corporation. These initial stockholders usually pay the par value per share for the shares which they purchase from the corporation. They put this initial 'seed money' into the bank account you opened after obtaining the IRS tax ID number.

To try to make things simple, let us create an example. ABC Corporation is formed in Delaware with 1,000,000 shares authorized at a par value of $1.00 per share. Three people found the ABC Corporation: Mr. A, Mr. B, and Mr. C. Each of these men purchases from the corporation 100,000 shares of stock and pays $1.00 per share. Now, the corporation has 300,000 shares issued and outstanding and also has $300,000 cash in the bank.

Mr. A, Mr. B and Mr. C intend to go into the general business of producing widgets. Perhaps they start this new business right away or perhaps not. In any case, eventually they reach the point where the corporation needs more money.

Therefore, they decide that the corporation will sell more shares. Perhaps they find a fourth person, a Mr. D, and he buys shares from the corporation. However, there is another way. They can go to a stock broker and get him to agree to underwrite a 'new issue' of shares.

The stock broker who does this is called an 'underwriter'. What this word means is that he agrees to purchase all of the shares to be newly issued and agrees to resell them to the public. The underwriter guarantees the issuance and purchase of the shares. If he cannot sell them, he must eat them himself.

There are many different kinds of underwriter. However, it is now no longer necessary for the underwriter to promise to purchase all the shares himself. He can agree to become the underwriter on a 'best efforts' basis. This means that he will try his best to sell the shares, but makes no guarantees. This seems to be a contradiction in terms. By definition, an underwriter is one who guarantees the sale. However, no underwriter is willing to bear that kind of risk any more, so the meaning of the term itself has changed.

Mr. A, Mr. B and Mr. C go to the underwriter. They tell him that they want to 'go public' in the stock market. The underwriter, whose name is Goldman, Sachs, investigates their background and their business. If they have a good business plan, a good business reputation and no obvious skeletons in their closet, the underwriter might agree to sell their shares to the public.

Mr. A, Mr. B and Mr. C do not want to give the public the same deal which they gave themselves. Therefore, they agree to sell to the public the 700,000 remaining authorized but, as yet, unissued shares at $10 per share. This will give them $7,000,000, minus the underwriter's fees and commissions. After that, the corporation will have $7,300,000 in the bank, minus the expenses which it has already paid.

When they sell the shares to the public through the underwriter, they sell the 700,000 shares in 100 share lots. This means that 7000 different people will buy these shares in lots of 100 shares each.

Because of this, the ABC Corporation, which makes widgets, now has 1,000,000 shares authorized, issued and outstanding. It also has 7003 stockholders and it has $7,300,000 cash in the bank. Remember that this is only an example, by way of illustration. In real life, it can happen in many different ways.

Widget making is an uncertain business. Nobody can say for sure if widgets will become popular or not. Probably, only Mr. A, Mr. B and Mr. C are completely confident that the widget business will be successful. Otherwise, somebody else would have started this business earlier.

There is an old saying: 'It is a difference of opinion which makes a horse race.' Everybody has a different idea of how to make money in business. Most ideas fail. Only a few ideas succeed. However, those few ideas which succeed can change the course of human history.

What about the 7,000 people, each of whom purchased 100 shares of stock in ABC Corporation at $10 per share? Aren't they all confident that the widget business will succeed?

Actually, those 7,000 people probably do not know very much about the widget business, if indeed anything at all.

They bought the stock only because their stock broker advised them to buy it. At the same time, their stock broker does not know anything about widgets, or about anything else, for that matter. Their stock broker advised them to buy it, not because the stock broker had a genuine concern for whether they made money or not. Rather, he advised them to buy the shares of ABC Corporation because he was paid a fat commission by the underwriter to push these shares onto his customers.

The underwriter also took fees for selling the shares. However, the underwriter does sincerely want the widget business to be successful, even if he is not entirely certain of what a widget really is. He wants the business to be successful because, if the business is successful, his customers will make money and will also buy shares in the next company he decides to underwrite. An underwriter with a good reputation will make millions by selling shares in a string of company after company to the public. However, if just one company fails, the reputation of the underwriter will be ruined and nobody will buy shares in the companies he underwrites any more.

The ABC Corporation now has $7,300,000 cash in the bank. It uses that money to start making widgets. At first, sales are slow. The buying public is not completely convinced that what it really needs is a new widget. It will take a long time before anybody will really know whether this widget business will be successful or not. For example, who could possibly have imagined that it would have been possible to make a computer out of an apple? Similarly, nobody can know for sure whether widgets will sell, until somebody tries.

As time goes on, people have new ideas about whether the widget business will be successful or not. Some of those 7,000 people who bought their shares may want to sell. Perhaps, they want to sell because they have lost confidence in the widget business. However, it is much more likely that they do not even know, nor do they care, what a widget even is. They want to sell their shares because they want to go on a vacation, or they want to buy something else in the stock market.

They want to sell, but to whom? The ABC Corporation 'went public' by selling its shares through an underwriter. Now, that is over. The ABC Corporation is using the money it obtained from the sale of these shares to make widgets. It will probably never be willing to buy back the shares. Therefore, the public customer needs to find somebody else to buy his shares. Let us say, for example, that this public customer is a businessman who runs a small company in Kansas City, Missouri. He wants to sell his shares in ABC Corporation which he has purchased from Goldman, Sachs, but to do that he needs to find somebody who wants to buy. Where does he find that person?

At that very moment, there is, on the other side of the world, out in the river near Hong Kong, a little man furiously paddling his one-oar boat in the darkness of night trying to escape from the Mainland. This man knows exactly what a widget is. He has even figured out a way to make a widget faster, cheaper and better than any man in history has ever made a widget before. All he needs to do is to make it safely to the shore so that he can buy a majority of shares in a widget company and put his idea to use.

Therefore, we have one man, sitting in his air-conditioned

office in Kansas City, Missouri, U.S.A., trying to think of a way to sell his widget shares so that he can buy flowers for his mistress, make his latest alimony payments and still have enough money left to go play a round of golf. Then, we have the other man, noiselessly gliding through the river in the dead of night on the other side of the world, but he knows better how to make widgets. Now, the question is: How do these two men find each other?

The answer is: They both go to the stock market, and, through the stock market, they find each other.

The little man in the sampan crawls to the shore, sneaks past the refugee camp, gets his bearings and makes it to the money exchange office in Kowloon. There, he changes his Chinese Renmenbi for Hong Kong dollars, which he then plunks down in front of a surprised Chinese stock broker and says that he wants to buy 100 shares in ABC Corporation which, at that very moment, the other man in Kansas City wants to sell. The Chinese man wants to buy because he knows and believes in the future of widgets. The man in Kansas City wants to sell because he does not even know what a widget is, nor does he want to learn, either. He only wants to get some money quickly, so that he can go out and play a round of golf.

By now, the shares of ABC Corporation are traded in one central market place, somewhere in the world. That one central market place might be the New York Stock Exchange, the American Stock Exchange ('on the curb', as they say), on NASDAQ, in the 'pink sheets', on the Hong Kong Stock Exchange, or on any of a dozen other places. However, it is rare for any stock to be traded in more than one central market place. Almost always, there is one central market place where almost everybody who wants to buy or to sell shares in any particular stock goes. There might be other, smaller market places, but usually at those other places they 'trade around' the main central market place.

Let us say, just for example, that the shares of ABC Corporation are now traded on the New York Stock Exchange. The man in Kansas City calls his local Merrill, Lynch office and places his order to sell 100 shares of ABC Corporation at the market. The local Merrill, Lynch order clerk then sends the instructions to the Merrill, Lynch head office in New York City to sell the 100 shares. The next order clerk in the Merrill, Lynch head office relays the order to another clerk who is working on the floor of the New York Stock Exchange. That order clerk gives the order to the Merrill, Lynch floor broker, who then takes it out to the ring where the specialist who deals in all ABC shares is standing.

At just about the same time, the little Chinese man who, by now, is out of his sampan and is standing in stock brokerage office with his newly exchanged Hong Kong dollars clutched in his hand, tells his broker there that he wants to buy 100 shares of ABC Corporation at the market. That broker is probably not a member of the New York Stock Exchange, but nevertheless has a correspondent broker who is a member, and that broker clears through Spear, Leeds & Kellogg at 115 Broadway in New York City. Within minutes, the order to buy, after also passing through many hands, arrives at the Spear, Leeds head office in New York City. Soon, the Spear, Leeds floor broker is moving towards the same ring on the New York Stock Exchange to buy 100 shares for the customer in Hong Kong.

The two floor brokers, one from Merrill, Lynch, the other from Spear, Leeds, arrive at the ring of the specialist on the floor of the New York Stock Exchange at almost exactly the same time. Both ask the specialist for a quote on the market in ABC Corporation. The specialist says: '6 7/8ths bid, offered at 7 1/8'. Both floor brokers hear this quote. Both of them are holding a dozen orders in their hands, to buy and sell all kinds of different stocks. They have only a few seconds to devote to this one transaction. They quickly agree to a price of 7 and go on their respective ways. The Merrill, Lynch floor broker writes on his order slip that he sold the 100 shares to Spear, Leeds at 7. The Spear, Leeds broker writes on his slip that he bought 100 shares at 7 from Merrill, Lynch. They move on, as this will be only one of hundreds of transactions that each will do on this particular day.

The next question is: From where did the specialist get his quote: '6 7/8ths bid, offered at 7 1/8'?

The answer is: He got it out of his head! All day, every day, the same specialist is standing there in the same ring, buying and selling all the shares of ABC. Almost every share of ABC Corporation that is bought or sold anywhere in the world passes through that ring. The specialist knows every trade that has ever been made in that particular stock. He knows the supply and he knows the demand. He has a list in his pocket of every broker who wants to buy and the price per share that he is willing to pay for that stock. He also has another list of those who want to sell. When he gave the quote '6 7/8ths bid', that was the highest price that he knew about that anybody was willing to pay at that particular instant in time for 100 shares of ABC. Similarly, the quote of 'offered at 7 1/8' was the lowest price of anybody that he knew about who was willing to sell.

Usually, the buyers and the sellers with a fixed price in mind leave their orders with the specialist. Traditionally, if the specialist handled the resulting transaction, he got a brokerage fee of two dollars per hundred shares. From this came the term 'two-dollar broker', which is still in use today, even though the floor brokerage commission is now much higher. Two dollars per hundred shares may not seem like much, but it adds up when one does a thousand transactions like that per day.

This example only applies to the New York Stock Exchange. The American Stock Exchange has a different system, involving hand signals. The Pacific Coast Stock Exchange has yet another system. There is still another system for the over-the-counter market. However, all these systems work under the same basic principle. In all cases, no matter how far away the actual buyer and seller are, all transactions come together in one central market place.

Just to further illustrate how this works, there are some corporations which are so big that their shares are traded 24 hours a day around the world. A company like General Motors Corporation might be traded on the New York, the Pacific Coast, the London and the Hong Kong Stock Exchanges, plus several others. However, the main market will always be the New York. Under normal circumstances, nobody in Hong Kong is going to be willing to trade, unless he knows the last price in New York.

Sometimes, it happens that there is a serious snowfall on

Long Island in New York State. Many of the brokers who work on the floor of the New York Stock Exchange live out on Long Island, not to mention the order clerks and the other brokerage personnel. The market cannot function without these people. If the snow fall on Long Island is heavy, the trains stop running. If the Long Island Railroad stops running because of heavy snowfall, there is no choice. The New York Stock Exchange must close, even if not a single flake of snow falls on New York City itself. If the New York Stock Exchange closes, then the Pacific Coast Stock Exchange also closes. The London and Hong Kong Stock Exchanges will remain open for other business, but almost nobody out there in Hong Kong is going to take the risk of buying or selling any General Motors shares, without knowing the latest price in New York. Thus, a little snowfall only on Long Island is enough to shut down the entire stock market all the way around the world.

Still, there is one unanswered question, a question of utmost importance. The question is: What determines the price of 7?

Of course, the short answer is that the price was determined by the law of supply and demand. The highest bidder was willing to pay only 6 7/8. The lowest offerer was only willing to sell at 7 1/8. Therefore, the deal was done at 7.

However, the deeper questions are: What made the seller willing to sell at 7 1/8? Why was the buyer willing to pay 6 7/8?

This question requires a long answer. Originally, there were 700,000 shares of ABC Corporation sold to the public at $10 per share. However, at that point, the company had not made even one widget. Mr. A, Mr. B and Mr. C simply had a plan on how to make widgets. The plan was still on the drawing boards. They had never made even one widget themselves.

It is also even possible that Mr. A, Mr. B and Mr. C do not themselves know very much about widgets. There is, actually, in the whole world, only one man who really knows about widgets. However, that one man is still in the river near Hong Kong. He doesn't have any means to walk into the Goldman, Sachs head office in New York City and sell them on the idea of a company which makes widgets. However, Mr. A, Mr. B and Mr. C have a friend at Goldman, Sachs, and therefore they are able to do that.

Let us move away from widgets for a moment and imagine that ABC Corporation instead has a cure for the AIDS virus. How did they happen to obtain that cure? It happened like this: One day, Mr. A, Mr. B and Mr. C were sitting around a desk in an office, thinking of ways to make money. Then, Mr. A said: 'I have a friend at Goldman, Sachs. My friend says that if we can come up with a good stock market idea, he will get his firm to float a new issue of our stock in the stock market.'

So, the three men thought and they thought. Finally, Mr. B said, 'I have an idea. We will find a cure for AIDS. With our cure, everybody with AIDS will have no choice but to pay us $10,000 for our treatment. Those who can pay will live, and the rest will die. Look at all of the people with AIDS, and how rich we will get. The only problem is, we don't have a cure for AIDS.'

So, they thought and they thought. Finally, Mr. C said:

'Hey, I remember. I had an old buddy in college, and now he is a research scientist in a major laboratory. He told me the other day that they were working on a cure for AIDS.' Quickly, Mr. C gets on the telephone and calls his friend.

The only problem is: His friend has a Ph.D. in microbiology and is already receiving a high salary backed by a U. S. government grant to do AIDS research. His friend is not going to leave his company and give up his high salary to join this venture. However, he is willing to go out for a few drinks after work and discuss this idea in a bar.

Later on, Mr. C and his microbiologist friend meet in a bar somewhere in lower Manhattan. After being fully imbibed on several drinks, the microbiologist takes a paper napkin from the bar and draws an outline of how an antibody capable of killing the AIDS virus would work. This is all that Mr. C needs. The next morning, he runs to his secretary and tells her to type out a prospectus on his word processor. The secretary already did this last week for another company wanting to go public. She has the standard phrases and clauses already inserted into the hard disk on her word processor. All she needs to do is to substitute the details of the new idea for the details of the old idea on last week's public stock offering. The rest is what we call 'boiler-plate', standard clauses which apply to just about every company which wants to go public.

By now, Mr. C knows enough about the AIDS virus so that he can convince anybody who is not really an expert on this subject that he really has a plan to cure AIDS. If anybody asks him a question to which he does not know the answer, he secretly calls his friend in the research laboratory and gets the answer. Of course, he really does have a plan. His plan is that as soon as this company succeeds in going public and in raising the money, it will offer a higher paying job to his friend who is already doing AIDS research. Even if that friend is still not available, there are always scores of out-of-work researchers looking for a job and capable of working on this idea.

Mr. A, Mr. B and Mr. C get back together. Mr. C gives to Mr. A his draft of a prospectus for a company which will find a cure for AIDS. Mr. A takes this draft of a prospectus to his friend at Goldman, Sachs. The friend at Goldman, Sachs thinks that this is a wonderful idea. Everybody will want to buy stock in a company with a cure for AIDS, he and his colleagues all say. Before long, the corporation is formed. Securities salesmen are at work on telephones in boiler rooms all across America selling the new stock to their public customers. Eventually, it becomes a 'hot new issue' and the shares go way up in the open stock market.

The reader will say, 'There is something wrong this. They can't get away with that. They don't really have a cure for AIDS yet'.

That doesn't matter. What difference does it make that they never really found a cure for AIDS? The only thing that matters is that everybody made money. The public bought the stock and the stock went up. Almost all of the original customers of Goldman, Sachs who bought the stock in the original underwriting or in the open market sold their shares at a profit or, at least, had ample opportunity to do so. That is all that matters. Everybody made money. It will be years before the world ever knows whether this company will be able to find a cure for AIDS or not. At least you can be sure that they will be devoting these years to working on finding a cure for AIDS, as they must work if Mr. A, Mr. B and Mr. C want to avoid going to jail for stock fraud.

Perhaps, they will really find a cure. Indeed, in the history of the stock market, much stranger things have happened. Sometimes companies actually do achieve the things which they claimed that they were going to do, however remote the possibility originally seemed to be.

However, our actual example is a widget company. Mr. A, Mr. B and Mr. C do not actually know how to make a good, working widget. Also, the only man who does know is still in the river near Hong Kong.

After ABC Corporation went public with the sale of 700,000 shares at $10 per share, the stock starts going up and down. Perhaps, ABC Corporation starts making widgets successfully, or perhaps not. The ideas upon which ABC Corporation were founded might succeed, or they might fail. It will probably take years before the final verdict is in. Ultimately, a successful company is one which pays dividends to its stockholders. However, a new company in a growing field often will not pay any dividends at all but will use all the profits to expand its business. The companies which pay the highest dividends are often stodgy, old line companies, like General Motors, in a downward trend.

Take, for example, Xerox Corporation. That was a company with a new, untested idea for a photocopy machine. Most people never thought that this idea would work. Most of those who did think that this idea was possible felt that this was a new type of business which would never amount to much. There were just a few investors who believed that Xerox Corporation could actually make a photocopy machine and who also believed that such a machine would be popular and would bring the company a profit. That small minority of investors who believed in Xerox Corporation made a hundred times profit on their money, even though Xerox Corporation paid almost no dividends during this period of phenomenal growth.

This happens to be the favorite example of this author, because the author of this book, while still only 15-years old, bought one (!) share of Xerox Corporation on the very first day that it traded on the New York Stock Exchange way back in 1960, and made a big profit on it. He read about it on the Dow Jones News ticker just a few hours before trading started on the New York Stock Exchange for the first time. The price he paid was exactly $106 per share. Within weeks, it was worth $250 per share, and that was only the beginning.

At the same time, for every example like Xerox Corporation, there are a hundred examples of companies with equally good-sounding ideas which never made it. This does not mean that the people who invested in those companies lost their money. In practice, the shares went up and down. Some investors bought low, sold high and made a big profit, even though the company eventually went out of business. The thing which makes Xerox Corporation unusual is that it did not obey the laws of gravity. It went up, stayed up, and is up to this very day, more than 30 years later. It made such a big profit during the 17 years when it had a patented monopoly on the making of photocopy machines, that it became permanently established as one of the major corporations in

America. Such cases are rare.

The main point is that often many years will pass before the final verdict is in. ABC Corporation goes public on the idea of making a better widget. It might make the widgets, but the widgets don't work. The widgets might work, but they don't sell. The widgets might sell, but the overhead cost might be too high. There might be a profit. There might be a loss. ABC Corporation might never make a single widget, but it might go into a totally different line of business which turns out to be a great success.

The point is that during the many years which may pass between the time that ABC Corporation goes public and the time when it can first pay a dividend, the shares will go up or down from day to day based upon whether the investing public believes that this will be a good business or not. The only thing which matters is the public opinion about this particular company. Whether the company actually makes a profit or not is a secondary issue.

There are many examples of companies whose profits increased, and yet the stock went down. There are an equal number of examples of companies whose profits went down or who suffered a loss, and the stock went up. In fact, as often as not, news about a stock causes the market to go in a different direction from that in which it should logically go.

This process is called discounting. ABC Corporation announces a record profit. The stock goes down. ABC Corporation announces a record loss. The stock goes up. Why is that?

There is a principle which explains this. That principle is: 'Buy on rumor, sell on news'.

The way it goes is this. Word speeds through the stock

market that ABC Corporation is about to make a major oil discovery off of the coast of Indonesia. However, nothing appears in the newspapers. The stock goes way up.

Two weeks later, the news comes out. ABC Corporation has discovered oil off of the coast of Indonesia. The story appears in the Wall Street Journal and on the Dow Jones News Tape. Immediately, the stock crashes.

Why is that? Actually, this is not a rare case. It almost always happens like that. As the old timers used to say: 'When good news appears on the tape, sell as much as you can. You will almost always make money. It's as easy as shooting fish in a barrel.'

Why is that? Don't you understand, Dummy? Everybody close to the company knew and all the analysts following it knew about the oil find in Indonesia. They bought shares in anticipation of the news release. When the news release came, they had no reason to keep holding their shares. The entire public knew what they knew, so they all sold at once. A few stupid people bought, thinking that the good news meant that the stock would go up, but a far greater number of shares were held by those who knew the company in detail and who were ready to sell as soon as the news hit the wire, so the stock went down.

The shares of stock were bought through a stock broker. The stock broker is a bright and well-mannered young man who knows a great deal about the stock market. The reason that he knows so much about the stock market is that he once took a six months training course from his employer in how to sell securities. In addition, he has a college degree. It is this college degree which qualifies him as an expert in the stock market.

Your stock broker can provide you with useful information. When he tells you to buy a particular stock, you will know that that is the time to sell it. When he tells you to sell, you will know that that is the time to buy. Follow this rule, and you will almost always make money.

Why is that? The reason is that the stock which the stock broker tells you to buy is the one which his employer told him to push this morning. The reason that his employer told him to push that stock this morning is that this is the stock which his employer has too much of. The stock broker will even tell you that himself. He will say, 'We like this stock so much that we own it ourself.' Why, then, is he so anxious to sell it to you?

The stock market performs a basic function, which cannot be performed in any other way. There are 50,000 companies in America with shares traded in the market. There is no way that anybody can possibly know for sure whether any one of them will be successful or not. There is no absolute way to determine what the value of these shares will be. No governmental agency could possibly pass a law or any just rule fixing the value of these shares. Instead, the shares will go up and down in accordance with the law of supply and demand.

The investor who buys these shares has no way of knowing whether they will go up or down. However, he does know one fact of utmost importance. He knows that one week or even one month from now, there will still be a market for these shares. He will still be able, no matter what happens, to go to his stock broker and sell these shares at a price. The price might higher than what he paid, or it might be lower. That is not the point. The point is that he will always be able to get out, even if it means taking a loss. In other words, his shares will be liquid.

This liquidity is of utmost importance. If there were no liquidity, if the investors in a new issue were not allowed to sell but were required to wait for many years until the company paid a dividend, almost nobody would be willing to invest in a stock on the stock market.

Chapter Five

Learning About the Rules

The foregoing chapters have all been elementary. To some, they might almost seem childish. Some readers will say, 'Why bother us with this. Everybody knows this already. Let's get to the serious stuff.'

Actually, a lot of people didn't know all this already. Many investors who have been 'playing' the stock market for years and who think that they know a lot about it, do not really understand even what a share of stock is. In fact, it is not really necessary for them to understand what a share of stock really is, in order for them to make money in the stock market. What they need to know are only the most simple concepts that the market for shares goes up in anticipation of future profits and dividends and goes down in anticipation of future losses. The exact mechanism of what causes this to happen is something which is useful to know, but this knowledge is not entirely necessary to the success of an investor.

However, one who wishes to conduct a successful corporate raid to take over a public company will need to know about a wide variety of different subjects. That is what this book is supposed to be about. That is why some elementary instruction was deemed necessary.

Now, we get to the good part.

Every one of the 50,000 companies which are traded in the

American stock market are traded either on the New York Stock Exchange, on the American Stock Exchange, on a regional stock exchange, or in the over-the-counter market. Shares traded in the over-the-counter market are traded either on NASDAQ or in the pink sheets.

Generally, the biggest companies are traded on the New York Stock Exchange, and the smallest are traded only in the pink sheets. The 'pink sheets' are so named because pink was the cheapest color of paper back when the pink sheets were first printed.

There are also companies which are not even listed in the pink sheets. Some companies have lost their listing in the pink sheets and are not traded there. Some have never been listed there, or anywhere else, for that matter. Their shares are not publicly traded, but they are sometimes nevertheless publicly held by a large number of stockholders.

An example of this is a California company named Science Applications, which is believed to do spy work for the C.I.A. I discovered this company myself many years ago, after an exhaustive search I conducted of every public company which had never even been listed in the pink sheets. I thereafter put their name in the pink sheets for the first time myself (actually I used my Latvian wife as a front), and they got really angry about that, because I blew their cover.

The 50,000 publicly held companies can be divided into the 'reporting companies' and the 'non-reporting companies'. The reporting companies are those companies which are required to file reports with the United States Securities and Exchange Commission under Section 12(g) of the Securities Exchange Act of 1934.

The United States Superintendent of Documents has for sale a handy rule book which explains this. The name of this easy-to-read volume is: *Code of Federal Regulations, Vol. 17, Part 240 to End.*

Fear not. It is only 805 pages long, with 10-point type. It can be had for a price of only about $23.00 by writing the Superintendent of Documents, Washington, D.C. 20402. If you are serious about this, rush out and buy one right away.

There is also a Superintendent of Documents Bookstore in the lobby of 26 Federal Plaza in New York City, among other places. In addition, this volume can be found in almost any local law library in the United States dealing with federal law. You can steal one from almost any federal courthouse and take it home. Nobody will notice that it is missing. In addition, this will be good practice for your future corporate raid.

There are two major laws of the United States which deal with publicly held securities. These are the Securities Act of 1933 and the Securities Exchange Act of 1934. These laws are constantly being amended and updated. The latest amendment to the Securities Exchange Act of 1934 took place on July 1, 1991. Almost nothing remains of the original 1934 law.

In general, the Securities Act of 1933 deals with the new issuance of shares to the public, which usually occurs through a public underwriting. The Securities Exchange Act of 1934 concerns what happens to the shares after they have been issued and sold to the public. Since the title to this book is *How to Take over an American Public Company,* we are only concerned here with companies whose shares are already publicly traded. Therefore, we are concerned only with the Securities Exchange Act of 1934.

It is possible to obtain a free copy of these acts from the Public Reference Rooms of the S.E.C. in Washington, D.C., in New York, in Chicago and in Los Angeles. You can also call the Public Reference Room of the S.E.C. in Washington, D.C. at (202) 272-7460 and try to get them to send you a free copy in the mail.

The section of the Securities Exchange Act of 1934 which deals with take-overs and tender offers in the stock market is known as the Williams Act, so named for the famous United States Senator, Harrison Williams, who was indicted in a stock fraud scheme and forced to resign from the Senate. In one of the great ironies of securities history, he was found to have violated his own law.

Of course, I never liked Senator Harrison Williams, because he pushed through many of the laws which the S.E.C. is always chasing me around about.

The sections of the Williams Act which cover tender offers are Section 13(e), 14(d) and 14(e) of the Securities Exchange Act of 1934. The rules of the S.E.C. under those acts are rules 14d-1 through 14d-101 and rules 14e-1 through 14e-4. There are also Section 13(e) rules, but these are not important to this book, because those rules only concern companies which are buying back their own stock. Here, we are concerned only about companies buying stock in other companies.

There is one important thing to remember about all of these laws and rules. This is: **These laws and rules work to your advantage.**

Why is that? The reason is that without these laws and rules, you would never be able to take over an American public company. Most of these laws and rules were just passed in their present form within the last few years. Their immediate effect was that take-overs suddenly became popular.

It is because of these changes in the law that it has now become relatively easy to take over an American public company. This is the reason that these take-overs have only become popular in the past few years. All of these rules work to the advantage of the outsider trying to get in. The entrenched management of a major corporation forms a big target which can be shot down with a small gun. Even that little Chinese man, still in the river near Hong Kong, could take over a major American public company, if only he could avoid getting caught in a refugee camp and then obtain a good Chinese translation of the *Code of Federal Regulations, Vol. 17, Part 240 to End* and understand how to put it to use.

Therefore, what you must do is this: **You must obey the law.** The reason for this is because it is the morally right thing to do.

Actually, there is a second reason. That second reason is that your opponent is not going to obey the law. The reason for this is that he is not going to know what the law is. All that man will know is how to make a profit in his business. He foolishly thinks that this is enough. He is not going to run out and buy a copy of the *Code of Federal Regulations, Vol. 17, Part 240 to End.* He is not going to read this book. Instead, he is going to hire a lawyer. That lawyer is going to charge him a lot of money, but that lawyer is going to be lazy. That lawyer is going to tell him the first thing which pops into his head, without bothering to read the rule book. You are going to take over his company, because you know the rules and he does not.

There is a popular new movie which came out about this. It is aptly called *Other People's Money* and is staring Danny De Vito, Gregory Peck and a beautiful young girl who plays the lawyer. Everything in that movie is exactly right and could happen just like that. Whoever was the technical adviser for that movie knew the rules. For example, when Danny De Vito says: 'File a Schedule 13D on this right away', that is exactly the schedule which needs to be filed in that situation. You will find out what a Schedule 13D is by the time that you finish reading this book.

Later, the girl lawyer says that the rules should be changed to put people like Danny De Vito out of business. To this, Danny De Vito replies, 'If you change the rules, you don't put us out of business. We adapt.'

I am going to refer to that movie several times throughout this book. The reason for this is that it useful to do so. I assume that many more people will see that movie than will read this book. In fact, this book will so closely follow the movie that the reader might even think that I got the idea for this book from that movie. However, I was doing this long before that movie ever went into production.

If you don't believe me, try searching for my name under the Lexus Securities Law Computer Network. You will find at least 31 federal securities cases with my name on it, going back to 1971 and going right up to the United States Supreme Court. You will also be able to find out what Chief Justice William Rehnquist personally thinks about Samuel H. Sloan.

Some of these remarks about me are not entirely flattering. Just to cite one example, here is what you will find in the law books that the United States Court of Appeals for the Second Circuit, regarded as the second highest court in the United States of America in the field of securities law, had to say about me back in 1976: 'This is Mr. Sloan's latest maneuver in his long struggle to avoid compliance with the Securities Exchange Act of 1934 and the rules and regulations of the S.E.C. promulgated thereunder.' *Sloan v. S.E.C.*, 547 F.2d 152 (2d Cir. 1976).

In reality, this remark was highly unfair and prejudicial. Even back then, I was complying with the rules, but my opponents were not. Nevertheless, nobody will dispute the fact that a great part of the body of the federal securities case law was made by me.

Now, for the first time ever, I am going to reveal to people like you how to do it.

Chapter Six

A Closer Look at the S.E.C.

The Securities and Exchange Commission was created as a result of the Securities Exchange Act of 1934. The first Chairman of the Securities and Exchange Commission was Joe Kennedy, the father of future President John F. Kennedy. There is a famous quote about this. Somebody once asked President Franklin D. Roosevelt why he had appointed Joe Kennedy as the first Chairman of the S.E.C. in 1934. 'How could you possibly do a thing like that?,' was the question. 'Everybody knows that Joe Kennedy is a big crook.'

To this, Franklin D. Roosevelt replied, 'It takes a crook, to catch a crook.'

In reality, Joe Kennedy lasted only one year as Chairman of the S.E.C. Much later came William Casey, who continued the fine tradition of crooked Chairman of the S.E.C. I got along with Casey real well. He was the one who started the tradition of the S.E.C. using the American Taxpayer's money to chase me around when, in reality, I am one of the few honest people in this business. Later, Chairman Casey moved over to become the Director of the C.I.A. At least I got my revenge later on when several newspapers gave me the pleasant task of writing Casey's obituary when he died.

However, the biggest crook of all was Stanley Sporkin, Casey's right hand man. He was the Enforcement Chief of the S.E.C. He once commandeered a special helicopter, at

American taxpayer's expense, just to get me, before I could take a trip to Iceland. However, you don't have to worry about Stanley Sporkin any more. He is no longer the Enforcement Chief of the S.E.C. He is now only a United States District Court Judge, in the Washington, D.C. Circuit.

Chairman Casey was a consummate liar, the kind of man who would tell a lie when the truth would serve him better. I knew all about the true character of Casey long before Casey became famous for this in the Iran-Contra scandal as the Director of the C.I.A. However, nobody listened to me back then, nor do they now, for that matter.

However, there is a reason why I am saying all this, and the reason is not merely to get back at fundamentally dishonest and evil men like Casey and Sporkin. Men like Casey and Sporkin will naturally rise to the top in a system which is corrupt. The second point is that any system which is controlled by the government has a natural tendency to become corrupt. As long as you have a Rajiv Ghandi or somebody like that sitting at the top, who has the power to decide who gets to go into business and who does not, it will almost always happen that the system becomes corrupt.

In other words, the only guarantee against corruption is the free market system. A just system must be one in which everybody can enter, and where everybody has the same chance to get on top. That little man, still in the river near Hong Kong, has every right to be able to take over IBM Corporation and run it better, if only he can focus his considerable brain power on how to do it.

Regarding the S.E.C., I am forced to admit that they are much more honest than they used to be back in the bad old days, or perhaps I have simply mellowed. Nowadays, some lawyers who used to work for the S.E.C. will freely admit that in those days they were taught and trained by Casey and Sporkin always to lie and to prevaricate when appearing before a judge in federal court. The S.E.C. staff lawyers were actually required to sit in classes taught under Casey and Sporkin where they were trained in how to lie. In short, they were trained to behave just like Casey and Sporkin themselves behaved. One attorney, still working for the S.E.C., once told me that in those days, the initials S.E.C. stood for 'See Everything Crooked.'

One especially crooked attorney I encountered in those days was a man named Willam Nortman. It is difficult to know how to react to a person when you see him telling a blatant lie without blinking, under circumstances where you know that he knows that you know that he knows that you know that he is lying. However, Nortman, like most of the others, is no longer with the S.E.C.

In short, my recent experience has been that the S.E.C. is much more honest than it used to be. I like to give myself part credit for that. Perhaps, they got more honest after I beat them several times decisively in federal court. However, I was not the only one who beat them. It is said that Harvey Pitt, the S.E.C. attorney whom I beat 9-0 in the oral argument before the United States Supreme Court, actually lost 17 cases in a row like that. His reward for losing 17 cases in a row is that Harvey Pitt is now one of the most respected securities lawyers in America.

Why did Harvey Pitt lose 17 cases in a row? The reason is because Harvey Pitt always took the most extreme position.

'The S.E.C. has the right to do everything. It can shut down every business. It can stop every trade. It can prosecute everybody. The public must be protected. Nobody can do anything at all, without the permission of the S.E.C.' This is what Harvey Pitt would always say.

Fortunately, enough federal judges realized that if they listened to Harvey Pitt, they all might as well go and live under the enlightened leadership of Chairman Brezhnev. This is the reason that Harvey Pitt lost 17 cases in a row. After that, Harvey Pitt left the S.E.C. and set up his own private law practice. Now, he has become the attorney for well-heeled corporate clients, lured into the belief that Harvey Pitt knows something about federal securities law. They think that Harvey Pitt knows something about securities law because his name appears right there in the law books as the lawyer on 17 major securities cases. They keeping overlooking the fact that Harvey Pitt lost all of those cases.

Anyway, if the reader of this book decides to act on it and needs a lawyer, go hire Harvey Pitt. His name can be found somewhere in the Washington, D.C. telephone book. He will be most happy to take your money. Be sure to tell him that Sam Sloan sent you.

Chapter Seven

Picking the Right Target

Now, the question is: How to Take Over an American Public Company. That is what this book is supposed to be about. Let us start from the beginning.

The thing to keep in mind is that there are 50,000 American public companies. There are all kinds of companies. Some are big. Some are small. Some are rich. Some are bankrupt. Some have assets. Some do not.

The most important point is: Some are fully reporting 12(g) companies. Some are not.

What is a 12(g) reporting company? Remember, I told you a long time ago to go to your local federal law library and steal a copy of *Code of Federal Regulations, Vol. 17, Part 240 to End*. You didn't do that yet. If you had done that, you would not have needed to ask that question.

A 12(g) reporting company is one which is required under Section 12(g) of the Securities Exchange Act of 1934 to register with the S.E.C. because it has more than $1,000,000 in assets and more than 500 stockholders of record.

Now, if you will just turn to page 102 of your handy volume of *Code of Federal Regulations, Vol. 17, Part 240 to End*, you will see that under Rule 12g-4 of the S.E.C., a company, once registered, can de-register, if the number of stockholders of record falls below 300. This is important.

The reason that this is important is that if you do succeed

in taking over an American public company, the first thing that you are going to want to do is to file a Form 15 with the S.E.C. This filing will cause the company to become de-registered with the S.E.C. pursuant to Rule 12g-4, provided that the number of stockholders of record has fallen to below 300 as a result of your take-over.

The reason for this is that companies registered under Section 12(g) are required to file audited 10-K annual reports and 10-Q quarterly reports with the S.E.C. These annual and quarterly reports tell everything about the business of the company. It costs these 12(g) companies a minimum of about $50,000 per year to have these reports prepared, usually with the assistance of a 'Big Eight' accounting firm.

It is virtually a requirement that every 12(g) reporting company must hire a Big Eight accounting firm to prepare its annual certified audit which must be filed on Form 10-K with the S.E.C. The reason for this is that only the Big Eight accounting firms will be willing to undertake such an audit. Only those firms have liability insurance against stockholder's suits, should their audit fail to uncover some material information about the company. The large number of multi-million dollar court judgments entered against the leading accounting firms in recent years demonstrate the reason why no accounting firm without a strong insurance policy is willing to undertake an audit of a 12(g) reporting company.

Only the Big Eight accounting firms can now get this type of insurance. The $50,000 fee which they charge for an audit, even to a small company, is used primarily to pay the insurance premiums on their liability insurance. This also means that if you are able to cause the company to de-register pursuant to Rule 12g-4, you will, by that action alone, save the subject company $50,000 per year.

Companies registered under Section 12(g) are required to send a copy of their 10-K and 10-Q reports to everybody who requests it. This is an important piece of information. This means that if you have a competitor in the United States and you want to know everything about his business, all you have to do is write him a letter and ask him to send you a copy of his latest 10-K and 10-Q reports. He is required by law to send them to you.

That bit of information can be easily worth many times the price of this book.

I once did a mailing in the following manner: I obtained from the S.E.C. a list of the name and address of every company which is registered with the S.E.C. under Section 12(g). Then, I mailed a letter to each of these several thousand companies, asking them to send me a copy of their latest 10-K and 10-Q report. The response was unbelievable. Every day, the United States Post Office dispatched a special mail truck only to bring the mail which I was receiving that day to my house. I actually opened these envelopes and sorted and cataloged all of this mail. This is how I discovered the stock, Science Applications, which is actually a front for the C.I.A. However, eventually my entire house became filled up with all of this stuff. I had to pay a special garbage truck to come and take it all away. This all happened in 1978.

There is now a better way to do this. An example of this can be seen in the movie: *Other People's Money*. At one point, Danny De Vito says: 'Mirror, Mirror on the wall. Whose the fairest of them all?' With that, he logs into his computer. The answer comes back: New England Wire and Cable. Danny De Vito then runs out and starts buying shares in New England Wire and Cable.

Danny De Vito was able to do this because he had a computer modem. This computer modem was connected to a stock market information retrieval service. Information about every 12(g) reporting company was available from that service. After that, all Danny De Vito had to do was to ask the computer to search for a certain type of company. Danny De Vito was looking for a cash rich company with undervalued assets. He wanted to find a company which was trading at much less than the value of its assets upon liquidation. There are thousands of companies which meet that criteria which are trading in the American stock market. However, Danny De Vito was searching for the fairest of them all. After a computer search, he found New England Wire and Cable, a company rich in assets, but doing a business which was obsolete and was losing money.

Again, this movie was exactly on point. You can do the same thing. Buy a computer and a computer modem. Subscribe to a stock market information retrieval service. Log in and start searching for the company you are looking for.

Actually, there is a problem with this. These stock market information retrieval services exist only in America. This information is probably not readily available in Japan. You will presumably have to call America and spend many hours on a long distance telephone hook up.

This is another subject which is changing rapidly. If this information is not already available in Japan at reasonable cost, it probably will be soon. Dun & Bradstreet reports are already available on a same-day basis in Japan, as Dun & Bradstreet has an office in Tokyo, with a direct computer link to America.

Meanwhile, it is still possible to use the stone age method of writing a letter to every company which interests you and asking them for a copy of their latest 10-K and 10-Q report.

The main point is that there are 50,000 companies to choose from. With such a large selection, every kind of company is available. However, not all of these 50,000 are 12(g) reporting companies.

You will probably want to concentrate on 12(g) reporting companies for several important reasons. First, all 12(g) reporting companies are required to comply with the S.E.C.'s tender offer and proxy rules. Non-reporting companies are not required to comply with these rules. It is by operation of these rules that you have a big target to shoot at. Without these rules, it would be difficult or even impossible for you to take over an American public company. This is the reason why you must comply with all of these rules. The rules benefit you, the outsider, but you will not realize this benefit unless you comply with these rules.

Before deciding to take over an American public company, you must have a plan, an objective. You must ask yourself the following question: Why do I want to take over a public company? What do I hope to achieve?

This is an important question. The answer is not obvious. Some people want to be famous. Some people want to be rich. Some people have an idea on how to run the business better. Some people want to acquire the assets. There are all kinds of reasons which one might have for wanting to buy an American public company.

For example, suppose one wants to become famous. A good way to do that would be to buy a baseball team. Some baseball teams are traded in the stock market. The owner of a baseball team will automatically become famous, because of the many fans who like to watch baseball.

Just to take any random example, try to buy the Seattle Mariners. This will make you famous, even if your plan fails and you are not allowed to buy the team.

Another way to become famous would be to buy a big media publication, like the *New York Daily News,* which is the largest newspaper in terms of circulation in America. That would be easy to buy. It is for sale right now. The last owner fell off his yacht and drowned in the Atlantic Ocean. If you buy the *New York Daily News,* everybody will know that you are rich.

You will not be rich for long, however. The *New York Daily News* loses money at the rate of one million dollars per year. That is the reason why it is so easy to buy.

Buying the Seattle Mariners or the *New York Daily News* would not really be a business deal. It would simply be a way to gain media exposure. Real businessmen do not want media exposure, except in certain kinds of businesses. Real businessmen do not want anybody to know how big or how important they really are. For one thing, real businessmen are afraid that their children will be kidnaped by Christian religious fundamentalists seeking donations to their church. This is a big problem in America right now.

We know of exceptions to this general rule. Everybody has heard of Lee Iacocca, the Chairman of Chrysler. Isn't he a real businessman?

Of course he is. However, how many people can tell you the name of the Chairman of General Motors or of Ford Motors, both of which are much bigger than Chrysler Corporation? Nobody knows about them, except for a few industry stock market analysts.

Lee Iacocca has a good reason for wanting to keep his name in the news all the time. His company is broke and is on the verge of going out of business. If that happens, there will be only two car markers left in America. Lee Iacocca has to keep talking about this all the time, asking for tax breaks and higher tariffs against Japanese imports. Otherwise, his company will go bankrupt. However, if he ever got a job with General Motors, he would shut up too, all of a sudden.

We will assume that your objective is not to get your name in the newspapers (although you will) but rather to do a real business deal, as done by real businessmen. Therefore, you need to have a business idea. The best idea is this: Look at the business which you are in already. That is the business which you know better than anything else. Don't try to go into a business which you don't know. If you are not in a suitable business, try to find a business which you know almost everything about, or at least you know more than most people.

Now, look at all the companies in America which are in that business. Some of those companies will be making a product which you like better than others. If you like using an Apple Macintosh Computer, look at the company which makes them, and so on.

Remember that everything is for sale. Some things simply

cost more than others. I am not talking about an Apple Computer right now. I am talking about the company which makes Apple Computers.

Of course, it would cost a lot of money to buy the company which makes Apple Computers. However, never fear. You can always buy them with junk bonds. Americans love to turn in their perfectly good stocks and get junk bonds in exchange. Of course, later on, they cry like a baby when their junk bonds turn out to be junk. They will file a court case against you. They will claim that you failed to disclose to them that the junk bonds which you gave to them were junk.

Actually, Apple Computer is a bad example, because it is a high flying high tech stock. What you need is a low flying stock. You probably do not want to take over a good company which is fully valued by the stock market. You probably want to take over a bad company trading at a low price, which you can make better.

In the particular case of Apple Computer, there are 13,000,000 shares outstanding and it trades at about $65 per share. This gives it a total market valuation of $845,000,000 (eight hundred forty- five million dollars). Apple Computer has a good product, but that product is not worth $845,000,000. The idea of trying to take over this company has to be rejected immediately.

The point is this: You almost certainly do not want a high technology company. They are too expensive. You want a low technology company. They are cheap. This is the reason why, in the Danny De Vito movie, the company he chose was New England Wire and Cable, a company with very low technology.

Let's take for example, Sovran Bank. Sovran Bank is a sleazy bank in Virginia which is engaged in the regular business of stealing the life savings of elderly retired people. Sovran Bank has gotten to be a big bank, just by stealing old people's money. Of course, a bank like that has a lot of liabilities. What Sovran Bank does is that it calculates that the old people will die before they can get their money back. However, what happens if the old person lives, and sues them successfully?

In short, Sovran Bank is a can of worms. Nobody in their right mind would want to take over a bank like that. However, I will use them as an example anyway, because I happen to know a lot about Sovran Bank.

The first thing you do is to write a letter to Sovran Bank asking them to send you their latest 10-K and 10-Q reports. You read and study these reports, in detail. Remember, if you want to do this seriously, you must know more about Sovran Bank than Sovran Bank knows about Sovran Bank. Fortunately, this is not that difficult. Mr. Blow Dried, the Chairman of Sovran Bank, probably knows very little, if indeed anything at all, about the banking business. That is the way it is in America these days. If he knew something about the banking business, he would not feel the need to go out and steal old people's money.

You first look at the balance sheet of Sovran Bank. You will see that it has $44,000,000,000 in assets. 'Forty-four billion dollars!', you say. 'This is a big bank, four times bigger than BCCI. How do you expect me to take over a bank like that.'

Keep reading, and the truth will be revealed unto you.

You get down to the place where it says 'Retained Earnings and Net Worth'. You will see there that the net worth of Sovran Bank is $2,000,000,000. 'Two billion dollars', you say. 'That still sounds like a lot of money to me.'

Then, your eyes move up to the place on the page to where it says: 'Commercial Real Estate Loans Outstanding --- $32,000,000,000.'

'Commercial Real Estate Loans', you say. 'Didn't I read something about that. It seems that I read in the newspaper somewhere that most of these commercial real estate loans were no good.'

Quickly, you agile mind starts to work. 'Let's see now. If I subtract $32,000,000,000 from $2,000,000,000, what do I get?'

What you get, Dummy, is minus $30,000,000,000. That's right! Sovran Bank is broke, bankrupt! Sovran Bank is insolvent to the extent of Thirty Billion dollars!

Now, it all becomes clear. The reason that Sovran Bank is engaged in the regular business of stealing the life savings of elderly retired persons is that Sovran Bank needs that money to keep afloat a little longer, before the final collapse.

Now that you understand the true situation, you think again about whether you really want to buy Sovran Bank. Who wants to buy a bank which is about to go bankrupt? Actually, there are some people who might want to do that. Sovran Bank does have a few things in its favor. It has a listing on the New York Stock Exchange. It has tens of thousands of depositors, none of whom obviously have read the Sovran Bank annual report, because if they had read that report, they would have pulled their money out right away. Thus, they have a docile group of dim-witted customers.

Of course, Sovran Bank also has $44,000,000,000 in assets.

However, if you take them over, you cannot exactly go out and spend all the money right away. This is a bank, subject to state and federal banking regulations. Also, you can be sure that the state and federal banking regulators are watching Sovran Bank carefully. They know what you know, that Sovran Bank is insolvent. Any moves to the deplete the assets will be looked upon with a jaundiced eye.

For these reasons, Sovran Bank would not be a good takeover target. Better try an easy company, like TWA. They are not merely insolvent on paper. They have officially filed for bankruptcy.

Anyway, I will continue to use Sovran Bank as an example, simply because I happen to know that example. I prefer to take the name of a real company, rather than to make one up. By the way, Sovran Bank changed its name in December, 1991 and merged with another bank of similar ilk, no doubt for reasons related to their insolvent status. Their new name is Nation's Bank. However, I will use the old name here anyway, because I have a particular reason to be interested in Sovran Bank.

We will just assume that for some reason which nobody can imagine, you have made up your mind to buy Sovran Bank. You look in the newspaper for the latest trades on the New York Stock Exchange and you find that it is trading around $10 per share (before the merger).

Next, you look in the latest annual report and find that there are 100,000,000 shares outstanding. You multiply $10 per share times 100,000,000 shares outstanding, and you come up with a round figure of one billion dollars.

The average investor who did not read the balance sheet

very carefully would not be able to understand why a company with a net worth of two billion dollars has a market valuation of one billion dollars. Of course, you know the reason. It is only a bookkeeping entry in the balance sheet which says that Sovran Bank has a net worth of two billion dollars. There is no allowance taken for the thirty-two billion dollars in bad loans.

In the case of Sovran Bank, there is really nobody in the world with the money to buy it. Of course, there are a few, very few, people in the world with one billion dollars. However, those who have one billion dollars would prefer to keep it. They are not going to throw their money away on a worthless investment like Sovran Bank.

Still, owning that bank should have some value. If you take over that bank, you might be able to do something with it. Probably, the best strategy would be smile stiffly as the new President of Sovran Bank. Try to collect on the $32,000,000,000 in bad loans. Do not make any more bad loans. Hope that something will turn up. And hope that the federal government will bail you out of trouble if and when the bank finally fails.

That is probably the best and only plan. This probably explains some unwanted newspaper publicity which Sovran Bank received when it came out that they have a policy of not making loans to people living in black neighborhoods.

However, remember the principle: Do not try to take over a company unless you know everything about the business which it is in. If you know the banking business, and if you study the balance sheet carefully, perhaps you will find something there which will save Sovran Bank from going into receivership. I don't know the banking business. I am just assuming that you know more about the banking business than I do.

In reality, the only person who would want to buy a bank like Sovran Bank would be another bank. For example, a Japanese Bank interested in expanding their customer base in order to gain a foothold in America might be willing to take over a bank like Sovran Bank, even if it meant sustaining a huge financial loss. The fact that Sovran Bank is insolvent could be turned to advantage. You could say to the federal government regulators, 'If you don't allow us to take over this bank, the bank will fail and the American taxpayer, instead of us, will have to bail out the depositors.' Also, with proper Japanese management, Sovran Bank might even become solvent again.

One way to buy Sovran Bank would be to issue junk bonds. Those who issue junk bonds prefer to call them high yielding investments. However, everybody knows what they really are. You might as well call them junk bonds. That way, when the investors sue you later on, you will be able to point out to the judge in court that you always said that these bonds were junk. Therefore, the investors cannot claim that they have been defrauded.

Therefore, you file a registration statement for an issue called: 'Sovran Bank Junk Bonds 32% of 2002'. You offer to exchange every share of Sovran Bank common stock for $12.50 principal amount of Sovran Bank Junk Bonds 32% of 2002.

What this means is that if an investor owns 100 shares of Sovran Bank common stock, you will give him $1250 principal amount of Sovran Bank Junk Bonds 32% of 2002. Every year, the owner of these new bonds will receive an interest check for $400. Also, in the year 2002, he will be paid $1250.

This sounds like a really good deal, except for one thing. Any bond which pays interest of 32% is not exactly guaranteed to make it until the year 2002. There is a high probability that such a bond will go into default. Still, some investors would prefer to have a bond like that, than to hold on to the equally risky common stock of a company like Sovran Bank.

In reality, Sovran Bank is a bad example, as was Apple Computer. Apple Computer is a high flying stock, not worth the price. Sovran Bank is a can of worms, valuable only to somebody already in the banking business. I have only used the example of Sovran Bank, because I happen to know them, and they know me too. If you try to open an account with Sovran Bank, be sure to tell them that Sam Sloan sent you. I was once one of their best customers, by the way, before they stole my mother's money.

The problem with finding a more realistic example is that I don't want to give away any secrets. I know companies ripe for a take-over, but I am working on those myself.

The company in the Danny De Vito movie, New England Wire and Cable, was really a perfect example, which was one of the reasons why I liked the movie. That company had once traded at $60 per share, but as the old time wire and cable business declined, the price went down. The old man who owned the company did not want to sell or to go out of business, out of a misguided loyalty to his employees. Therefore, the company lost money year after year. Because of losing money for ten years in a row, the stock was down to ten dollars per share, with 4,000,000 shares outstanding. Nevertheless, the company had cash and other assets worth $100,000,000, or $25 per share, which is why Danny De Vito wanted to buy it.

In fact, this example is realistic. It may seem surprising, but there are a number of companies exactly like that. Almost always, these are old line companies in uninteresting businesses like making wires and cables.

Where do you find these companies? Actually, this takes a lot of work. There are 50,000 public companies. You cannot investigate all of them. One way around this problem is to search by industry group.

Generally speaking, the best candidate for this is likely to be an obscure, almost completely unknown company. In other words, it should be a company with no sex appeal. Take Apple Computer. Now that is a company with a lot of sex appeal. Who can remember that it nearly went bankrupt in 1985. You don't want a company with sex appeal. The price of the stock will be too high.

Try a company like Continental Can. No sex appeal. Who would ever want to sit on your continental can? Try Pullman Railroad Cars. Corning Glass Works. Jones and Laughlin Steel. Forget about Xerox Corp. Too much sex appeal.

However, those are all famous companies which everybody has heard of. What you need is a company which nobody has heard of. That's it! My favorite company. Hugoton Gas Trust. Who ever heard of that? Only traded in the pink sheets and lucky to be there. Only market maker: Kirkpatrick, Pettis in Ohama, Nebraska. Who ever heard of them? Only one asset: Sitting on top of one of the largest fields of natural gas reserves in the entire world. Also, one of the highest dividend paying stocks in the market. (I hope that you buy Hugoton. I still own it.)

If only natural gas ever becomes popular again, Hugoton Gas is perfectly poised to let go with a big one.

If, however, Hugoton Gas is not the right stock for you, there are plenty of others to chose from. You will have to look at thousands of companies, one by one, to find exactly the company you want.

Taking over a public company is serious business. You have to be prepared to do a lot of work. If you are discouraged at looking at the balance sheets for a few thousand companies, just remember: This is only the beginning.

Traditional stock market analysts do not look first at the balance sheet of a company. They look first at the earnings statement. The logic is this: A company may have a lot of assets. However, what is the use of these assets, if the company is losing money? A famous case was Penn Central. It had a book value of $105 per share. Nevertheless, the stock went down to $10 per share and kept going lower. This would seem like a sure thing. Buy for $10 per share stock in a company worth $105 per share. Make an easy profit of $95 per share.

However, it didn't work like that. Eventually, Penn Central, the largest railroad in America, went bankrupt. The shares became worthless.

What went wrong? For one thing, the $105 per share represented the value of the railroad tracks. If Penn Central had been allowed to sell the railroad tracks and build luxury hotels on the underlying land, Penn Central stock would have been worth a lot of money. However, Penn Central could not sell the railroad tracks. It was a government regulated monopoly. Therefore, the land to which it gave such a high value could not be sold and therefore was worthless, for practical purposes.

There are many examples like this. For this reason, stock analysts were reluctant to give any consideration to book value per share. They looked to the earnings instead. They felt that the price/earnings ratio was a more reliable indicator of the value of a stock.

However, the price/earnings ratio is also a dangerous gauge to rely upon. For example, Bank of America just announced that it earned one billion dollars last year. However, the word on the street is that the Bank of America is in serious financial difficulty and could go 'belly-up' at any moment.

The truth is that there is no sure way to gauge the value of a stock. You can use handy indexes like the price/earnings ratio. However, this is like playing with a toy for children, which most stock market analysts really are. A serious investor who knows what he is doing reads everything about the stock before he invests. He especially reads the 10-K and 10-Q reports.

In addition, the Dun & Bradstreet reports should also be consulted. Dun & Bradstreet provides information of a different sort than the 10-K and 10-Q reports. The Dun & Bradstreet reports, among other things, provide information from suppliers as to whether the prospective target pays its bills on time or not, plus information regarding what liens and attachments there might be on the assets of the target corporation.

However, it is not enough to read everything about the stock itself. One must understand the entire industry and, indeed, the entire economy in which the company exists. In addition, there are intangibles. For example, we have already discussed the 'sex appeal' of a stock. A stock with good sex appeal will trade at a higher price/earnings ratio than the stock in a company with a low sex appeal. How do you factor in the sex appeal of a stock? Nobody can say for sure.

In any case, if you are interested in taking over a company and not in merely buying a few hundred shares as an investor, you need to look more at the balance sheet than at the price/earnings ratio. The logic in this is that under your new management, the company will be run differently, for better or for worse. The past earnings history will probably not mean as much as knowing what the company has left when you take over.

Getting back to basics, publicly held companies are traded on the New York Stock Exchange, the American Stock Exchange, a regional stock exchange, on NASDAQ, in the pink sheets, or not traded at all. A company which is not traded at all could still be the subject of a hostile take-over, as long as it is a 12(g) reporting company, but in no case in recent memory has that happened. Still, with research, a proper candidate company might be found.

The kind of companies which are best for taking over are heavy, cash rich, slow moving companies. Still, it seems shocking to learn that somebody was able to take over Gulf Oil Corporation, then the seventh largest company in the world. It was like a minnow swallowing a whale. There have been many cases like that recently.

The best candidates are probably not to be found on the New York Stock Exchange. The companies traded there are too big and too visible. Look for a small company which nobody has heard of.

After finding a suitable candidate, look at the balance sheet. To start off with, do a simple calculation. Find a recent stock price and also find out the number of shares outstanding. Multiply the two together. The result gives you the market valuation for the stock.

Now, look at the book value of the stock. That can be found under 'net worth' near the bottom of the balance sheet.

If the net worth exceeds or at least approximately equals the market valuation, you might have a potential candidate. However, this is only a minimal calculation. The balance sheet might have all sorts of hidden assets and hidden liabilities. This simple calculation is just a starting point for deeper research.

Some stock market analysts search for target companies for a different reason. They do not want to take over a public company themselves. Instead, they are looking for companies which are possible take-over candidates for other people. In other words, they are trying to predict which companies will be taken over in the future. They assume that if an attempt is made to take over a company, the price of the stock will go up.

Chapter Eight

Sizing Up the Opponent

It would be easy to write several books on the inexact science of picking a suitable take-over candidate. Therefore, we will just assume that you already have one. The question we keep evading is: 'How to do it.'

There are several ways to take over a public company. One is simply to purchase a majority of the outstanding shares in the open market. The second is through a tender offer. The third is through a proxy fight. Finally, all of the above can, and often are, combined.

Management can be expected to resist the take-over, for their own entirely selfish reasons. The existing chairman of the target corporation is probably drawing a fat salary to run this company. Salaries of one million dollars per year are no longer uncommon. Anybody with a salary like that is not going to take well to the idea of being thrown out of his job.

Since you can expect stiff resistance, you need to select a company where the management does not own much stock.

One reason why big companies are taken over more often than small, even though it takes much more money to take over a big company, is that in small companies the management is much more likely to own a large percentage of the total outstanding shares. It is common in small companies for the management to own 51% of the total outstanding shares. However, this is rarely true of large companies, for the simple reason that nobody has so much money.

Take, for example, American Telephone and Telegraph. The total market valuation for this company is more than 48 billion dollars. There are 1.3 billion shares outstanding and it trades at around $37 per share. Nobody could possibly own even five per cent of the total outstanding shares of this company. If he did, his shares would be worth more than two billion dollars.

Nobody has ever tried to take over American Telephone and Telegraph. It is simply to huge. There is a second problem. Any basic utility like AT & T is heavily regulated by the government. The government would have to pass upon any take-over attempt, and any outside take-over attempt would not likely be approved.

However, a non-regulated company like IBM could possibly be the subject of a take-over attempt, although that has never been tried either. The total market valuation of IBM Corp is more than 10 billion dollars.

If one company is buying another company in the same field of business, then there could be anti-trust considerations. For example, if a major steel manufacturer would try to take over another major steel manufacturer, there would definitely be an anti-trust problem. However, if a big computer company decided for some reason to buy a big coal mining company, there would be no anti-trust problem, regardless of how big each of the two companies might happen to be.

What would happen if a Japanese steel company decided to take over an American steel company? The answer is not readily available. As far as existing anti-trust law is concerned, it seems unlikely that there would be a problem. No doubt some Americans would argue that a vital industry like steel should not be allowed to fall into foreign hands. However, with steel being such a moribund and declining industry in America, any outsider who thinks that he can run the steel business better ought to be encouraged.

Regarding a foreign take-over, there are certain areas where America might be sensitive. Take, for example, the field of commercial real estate. This is a field in big trouble, with many defaults. A lot of big new buildings are right now for sale at much less than the cost of building them a few years ago. Somebody with enough money could buy one of these buildings for a relative song and wait until times get better (assuming that times ever do get better). It would be a mistake to try to buy the Empire State Building, however. Certain buildings are regarded as 'trophies' in the real estate business. This is because the person who buys such buildings is saying to the world, 'I am a rich man. I have money to throw away.'

There is a good reason for this conclusion. For example, the Empire State Building is an old, decrepit, run down building built in the depression era of the 1930's. It is sadly in need of renovation, which will never come because it would be too expensive. However, it is also one of the most famous buildings in the entire world. Anybody buying such a building would have to pay a premium over its real value. In other words, somebody buying the Empire State Building building would be buying it for the prestige value, not for the purpose of making a financial profit. This book is intended for people who are interested in making a profit, not for those interested in showing off.

If a Japanese consortium tried to buy the Empire State

Building, there would in all likelihood be a congressional investigation into this. This sort of thing should be avoided.

Nevertheless, there are no doubt much better buildings in Peoria, Illinois. Nobody will object if some rich Japanese wanted to buy one of those. There are so many and America can use the money.

Buying a building is different from buying a business. The owner of a building figures that he can wait until things get better. The owner of a business, if his product isn't selling, needs to cut his losses and get into a more profitable business right away.

Right now, the Japanese are concerned about what is known as 'Japan bashing'. There is news about this every day in the newspapers. The real problem is this: America has a balance of payments deficit. More money is going out of America than is coming in. That money is going to many countries of the world. It is going to Arabia to buy oil. It is going to Germany to buy German products. Probably, more money is going to both of those countries than to Japan.

The difference is that the money which America sends to Arabia and to Germany eventually comes back. The Arabs sell oil, but they also buy American products. A shaikh from Arabia will bring all of his wives for a vacation to American and spend a lot of money. Germany also buys American products. However, the money sent to Japan doesn't come back. It stays in Japan.

Each year, America sends nearly $40,000,000,000 to Japan which doesn't come back. Each year, the figure gets bigger and bigger. America can see that it simply cannot afford to be spending $40,000,000,000 every year on this. America is in trouble right now, even without this problem.

This is the reason why some Americans are calling for an absolute and total trade embargo with Japan. They especially want to ban Japanese cars and Japanese television sets. They feel that they can do business with every other country in the world, but they cannot do business with Japan.

It is a mistake to assume that America will object to a Japanese take-over of an American company. What they will look at are the numbers.

If, for example, a Japanese company builds an automobile plant in America, this is seen as a good thing.

If, however, after a few years, it becomes clear that almost all of the parts to make these automobiles come from Japan and that only the last stages of assembly take place in America and the entire purpose to having a plant in America is to take advantage of the fact that there is a lower tariff on automobile parts than on completed automobiles, then some questions will be raised about this.

From the American point of view, Japan needs to think more globally. Japan cannot simply look upon America as a place to sell its products. Even if Japan does start buying a few things made in America, that will not really solve the problem. A few aluminum baseball bats will not make any difference.

The problem from the American point of view is the constant and unremitting outflow of capital from America into Japan, from whence it never comes back. Money which is sent to Japan is like money which is sucked into a black hole. Once that money is gone, it will never come back. At the same time, money which is sent to every other country of the world does come back to America eventually.

For this reason, the various points and contentions that this trade imbalance exists because Americans are lazy, Americans are stupid, American cannot make products up to the standards of the Japanese, and so on, miss the point. All of this may be true, but the point is that America is broke. America just does not have the money to be able to send $40,000,000,000 to Japan every year, year after year. That is the reason that there is a considerable body opinion in America right now which says that there should be an absolute and total ban in America on all products made in Japan, for whatever reason.

It has been pointed out that the average Japanese worker works 2100 hours in a year, whereas the average American worker works 1900 hours and the average German worker works only 1500 hours in a year. Thus, the contention is made that if only the Americans would work that extra 200 hours, the trade deficit would disappear. However, this is simply not going to happen.

Japan needs to take this problem much more seriously than it has up until now. Japan tends to think of this as a matter of racial prejudice. This is not the case. America also has a trade imbalance with China, with Korea, with Taiwan and with many other countries of the world. However, the imbalance is small, in most cases less than 5% of the overall trade. A difference of 5%, even over a long period of time, will not hurt America much. However, in the case of Japan, what Japan sells to America is double what America sells to Japan. There is no other country in the world like that.

In addition, what little that Japan does buy from America

consists almost entirely of natural resources, especially oil, which Japan does not have. Japan buys oil from the North Slope of Alaska, because Alaska is close to Japan. This does not do America any favor. America could sell that oil at the same price to anybody on the world market. What America wants is to be able to sell to Japan manufactured products made by American workers. America wants to be able to sell the type of products which provide jobs to the American assembly line workers who make them. In particular, America wants to be able to sell to Japan cars and television sets, the same products which Japan sells to America.

America does not believe the Japanese contention that American cars and television set are no good. America points out that in third countries in places like Europe and the Middle East, where Japanese and American cars compete on equal terms, the American cars often sell better.

The economic trade figures bear that conclusion out. The latest figures show that 66% of the entire world-wide trade deficit of the United States of America is with just one country: Japan.

A 50% or 100% trade imbalance with Japan cannot be politically sustained. Right now, George Bush is in trouble. He knows that he could easily lose the presidency solely because he is perceived as being 'soft on Japan'. He lost his strongest issue, which was the cold war, when the Soviet Union self-destructed. If the Democrats get in, it is entirely possible that they will decide to shut down all imports from Japan altogether. In fact, this might have been done years ago, except that it is illegal under existing American law to discriminate against imports from one nation.

It is only because of the restrictions imposed by American law and by the rulings of the American courts that America argues about silly things like rice, oranges and aluminum baseball bats, when the real issues are cars, computers and television sets. However, laws can be changed. Indeed, it will be done eventually, as long as the trade figures continue in their present trend, for the simple reason that America does not have enough money to sustain that level of constant outflow of capital to Japan.

On the other hand, if Japanese investors start buying up American companies, that would overcome the objections by the U.S. Congress. As long as these companies continue to operate in America and to provide jobs to Americans, nobody will care who the actual owners are. This will also tend to reduce the level of capital outflow to Japan.

The main point is that it is most unlikely that there would be an objection to a Japanese take-over of a middle-sized American company. Where the objection would come would be if Japan tried to take over a major industry, like General Motors Corporation, for example, or a major defense contractor, like Northrop Corporation or Lockheed Aircraft. This would certainly raise eyebrows.

If, on the other hand, a Japanese company decided to buy Bantam Books or Dell Comic Books or Fredericks of Hollywood (which makes ladies undergarments) or Camel Manufacturing or some other company in a non-essential field, nobody would object, even if it was the Russians who wanted to buy it.

In short, there are 50,000 public companies in America. Among these, there are probably not more than a few dozen to which there would be any objection to a foreign take-over. That still leaves more than 49,000 companies to chose from.

Chapter Nine

The First Financial Commitment

The first step to taking over a public company is usually to acquire a small number of shares in the open market. This should be done so as not to disturb the market. Let's say, for example, that the stock is trading at $10 per share. Every day, you put in an order to buy some shares. You should place your order to buy at 10 1/8.

Why is that? (I have a daughter who always says 'Why is that?' That's why I am always saying, 'Why is that?').

The reason is that there will be a whole bunch of people waiting in front of you to buy the stock at exactly 10. They have called their broker and said, 'I like this stock. If it ever gets down to 10, buy as much as you can.' American people like round numbers, especially if the number is equal to their own IQ.

On the other hand, if you want to sell, place your order to sell at 9 7/8 or at 10 7/8. This way, you will be ahead of all of those people who want to sell their shares at 10 or at 11.

Keep your order to buy at 10 1/8 for several weeks. That way, you will gradually accumulate shares without disturbing the market.

If you ever get up to 5% of the total outstanding shares, you must file a Schedule 13D with the Securities and Exchange Commission within ten days.

One way to get around this would be to form a group.

Then, you and the other members of this group will all have a lot of free time to talk about this when you are in jail for this together. You are not allowed to form a group for the purpose of evading Section 13(d).

What you can do, however, is acquire 4.999% of the shares. You do not have to file anything. There is nothing wrong with this.

Once you pass 5%, you must file six copies of a Schedule 13D within ten days. This means that you have ten days during which nobody else knows what you are doing.

In other words, you wait like a tiger in the bushes. You quietly accumulate 4.999% of the total outstanding shares. Then, you jump in and you have ten days to eat as much stock as you can before anyone finds out what you are doing.

However, you must be sure to file a Schedule 13D with the S.E.C. on exactly the tenth day. Do not dare to be even one day late or early. Be sure to use Federal Express guaranteed afternoon (not morning) next day delivery.

Why is that? The reason is that this game is not played by school boys in short pants. You don't want anybody to know anything about what you are doing, until the last possible moment. That is the key to success.

Your Federal Express package containing your Schedule 13D should be addressed to Securities & Exchange Commission, Office of Filings, 450 Fifth St., N.W., Washington, D.C. 20549. (I didn't have to look that up; I have that address memorized.) You must also send one copy to the target company.

What will then happen is this: There is a private company called Disclosure, Inc. They have a representative stationed at all times in the Office of Filings of the S.E.C. They get one copy of everything that comes in. Within a few hours of arrival, or by the next morning at the latest, your filing will be in their database. Every stock broker in the entire United States of America and indeed in the entire world will be able to obtain a copy of your Schedule 13D, upon payment of a fee, perhaps $25. In addition, the daily S.E.C. News Digest, an official U.S. government publication, will carry a list of all Schedule 13D filings, including yours. Furthermore, a hard copy of your 13D filing with be encoded into a Disclosure, Inc. compact disk. Copies of that disk will be distributed to every Disclosure Inc. branch office in the United States, to service their local clients, which include every stock brokerage firm in America. Stock market analysts will read your Schedule 13D and try to determine what the significance of it is. Research firms will distribute charts and graphs to all of their clients throughout the world, reflecting your Schedule 13D filing.

In short, as we say in America, all hell is going to break loose as soon as you file that Schedule 13D. This is the reason why you waited until the last possible legal moment to file it.

Chapter Ten

Sail Close to the Wind

One lesson that you have just learned is that you must obey the law. However, you do not go one inch further than the law requires you to go. You do not file a Schedule 13D when you have 4.999% of the stock. You get your pocket calculator out, and you wait until you have exactly 5% of the stock. You do not file with the S.E.C. on the ninth day. You do not file on the eleventh day. You file on exactly the tenth day, in the afternoon of that day.

Remember: This is not a game for children. You are playing this game for real money. Nobody is going to give you your money back if you play this game and lose it.

An important point to remember is that you do not want to disturb the market. All this time, you have been buying this stock at 10 1/8, which is about the price at which it was trading before you started to buy. It is very important to stick to that price and not to cause the market to go up.

Eventually, however, you reach the point where you can no longer do that. For one thing, this takes time. You might have a special need to take over this company right away. You might be afraid that somebody else might do it first. You might want to skip this gradual accumulation phase altogether. However, for a variety of reasons, you must buy at least some stock, if only a few thousand shares, before you move on to the next stage.

You will have decide whether you can afford to sit and wait for a month or two quietly accumulating shares before you move on to the next stage. This all depends on your strategy and your particular reasons for wanting to buy this stock.

There are some cases where you can just sit and slowly buy the shares at 10 1/8 until you finally have a majority of the outstanding shares. Before starting this take-over plan, you should have studied the market trading patterns carefully. You should have known exactly how much stock the management has and how much is held by institutional investors, such as mutual funds. You should have tried to find out whether there is 'off-the-board block trading' in this stock. You should have learned whether there is significant trading in the 'third market' or the 'fourth market'.

The term 'third market' applies to trading between brokers of large blocks of stock which do not cross the floor of New York Stock Exchange. The buyers and sellers know each other, so they do not go to the floor.

The 'fourth market' is where the institutions trade among themselves without the benefit of a stock broker. Large blocks of shares in big companies are held by mutual funds, life insurance companies, pension funds and other institutions. They sometimes call each other directly and buy and sell among themselves, thereby saving on commissions. This is called the 'fourth market'.

These institutions are not allowed to operate in secrecy. Institutions are required to inform their own stockholders and investors about their securities holdings. As a result, research organizations collect this data and publish them in stock market information services. At one time, the best place to get this information was known as the *Vickers Book*. Nowadays, this information is available from numerous stock market information services. From these services, you should be able to get a good idea of who the big stockholders are in your target company. Needless to say, you should have already accumulated this data before you bought a share of stock in your target company.

If the stock in your target company is held by a lot of institutional investors, you can simply call them up directly and ask them how much they want for their shares. You can get your broker to do it, or you can do it yourself. The advantage to having your broker do it is that then nobody will know that you are the real buyer. On the other hand, you lose something by this. Calling the decision maker directly yourself gives you the chance to listen to him on the telephone while he makes his decision. For example, he might say resolutely, 'I have absolutely decided to sell my shares as soon as it reaches 10 3/4 and I have placed the order with my broker already.' On the other hand, he might pause for a long time and say, 'Well, if the stock gets up to 10 3/4, I might strongly consider the possibility of thinking about selling at that level provided that there is no improvement in the general economic indicators.'

If your Merrill, Lynch broker had called each of these two people, the message might come back, 'Will sell at 10 3/4.' However, by talking to these people directly yourself, you have learned that one money manager is firm about his price, but the other is not sure and his price might go up or down.

One thing for sure, though, is that all of them will have a

price at which they will sell. Here is one big difference between America and Japan and indeed one of the major sources of friction between the two countries.

In Japan, you have 'stable investors'. This means, in short, 'I'll buy your stock, and you'll buy mine'. The law in Japan is that companies cannot buy back their own stock. Therefore, they swap newly issued shares or use their excess cash to buy stock in other companies which they are on friendly terms with.

An outsider cannot break into this system. If an American businessman comes to Japan and starts calling up institutional investors offering to buy stock in their friend's company, they are simply not going to sell, at any price. In America, we have a term for this. It is called: 'Restraint of Trade'. In short, an arrangement which is absolutely illegal in America is virtually required by law in Japan.

In America, the institutional investor must sell to you, regardless of who you are, provided only that you pay his price. 'You say your name is Boris Yeltsin? You say that you want to buy our Boeing Aircraft? Fine, we will sell all of our shares to you at 51 5/8. No problem.' This is what the institutional investor will say.

He **must** say that. The reason is that he has a fiduciary duty to his stockholders or to the beneficiaries of his fund to maximize their profits. In other words, he must make money for them. If he doesn't, they will fire him and hire a new portfolio manager. He cannot say to the elderly retired persons who happen to be the beneficiaries of his fund that he refused to sell at a high price because his close personal friend happened to be the president of the company of whose stock his institution is the owner. If he refuses to sell the shares held by the institution at a good price, he could easily be sued by the beneficiaries of his fund. Therefore, he must sell, provided that the price is right.

This does not happen in Japan. That is the reason that America keeps complaining that Japan needs to open its stock market to outside investors.

If the stock in your target company is substantially owned by institutional investors, it might be possible to accumulate a majority of the outstanding shares just by contacting them. This happens all the time, but there is little publicity. Often, there is just a short news article in the Wall Street Journal announcing that ABC Corporation has acquired a controlling interest in XYZ Corporation, that the old president of XYZ has resigned and that a new president has been appointed by ABC. That's it. Short and simple.

As a general rule, institutions tend to invest only in big, well known companies, usually companies listed on the New York Stock Exchange. The reason for this is self-preservation. If a well known company like TWA files for bankruptcy, all the portfolio managers who invested in TWA will say, 'It's not our fault. How could we have known that a big famous company like TWA would file for bankruptcy?' They will probably keep their jobs.

If, however, one of them invests in a tiny, little company like Canadian Javelin, and that company goes belly-up, not only will the portfolio manager lose his job, but he might even be indicted by a federal grand jury if it can be proven that he took a bribe to buy Canadian Javelin stock. These things can and do happen.

If your target company is not listed on the New York Stock Exchange and is basically a small company with less than $100,000,000 in annual sales, there will probably not be much in the way of institutional holdings. Assuming that you already know that management does not own a large block of shares, what will probably be left is a company with a large number of small shareholders with an average of 100 shares each.

This creates the most interesting situation from the point of view of somebody attempting a take-over. In fact, this situation is really what this book is about.

Chapter Eleven

Deciding the Next Step

You have now established that your target company has a large number of small stockholders, each owning an average of 100 shares. You have also established that while management owns a large block of shares, it does not control 51% of the company. Institutional holdings are nil. You want to take over.

First, you accumulate some stock. As soon as you have more than 5% of the total outstanding shares, you must file a Schedule 13D within ten days and all sorts of alarm systems will go off. In this situation, you had better move quickly. There are a wide variety of actions which your target company might take to prevent you from taking them over. You have to expect almost every dirty trick in the book, plus a few which are not even in the book yet. Once you are committed and there is no turning back, you must move quickly.

At about this time, you contact the target company. You call up the chairman on the telephone. You might ask to meet him, or you might break the bad news to him over the telephone.

The bad news will be that you have decided to take over his company, and to throw him out on the street. However, you will not put it exactly like that.

What you might say to him is something like this: 'Mr. Jones. Allow me to introduce myself. I am the Chairman of

ABC Corporation. In consideration of our over-all investment strategy, we have concluded that the stock in your company would make a suitable investment. A meeting of our board of directors took place this morning and, after due deliberation, we approved the acquisition of your corporation. We would like to arrange with you a meeting as soon as possible, to discuss the terms under which you would be prepared to sell. I must inform you frankly that we have already purchased 10% of the total outstanding shares of your corporation, and we will be filing a Schedule 13D with the S.E.C. at about 4:45 this afternoon.'

There are several obvious possible reactions to such a telephone call. One might be that he will say, 'We're not selling,' and slam down the telephone. However, he has to be careful, and probably he will not do that. More than likely, once he realizes that you really do own 10% of the total outstanding shares of his corporation, he will agree to meet with you promptly.

It must be pointed out that regardless of his personal feelings on the matter, he has a legal obligation to his stockholders. If you are prepared to offer him $100 per share, and his stock is only trading at $10 per share, then naturally he must accept your offer. On the other hand, if you are offering him $11 per share, then naturally he can refuse on the grounds of inadequate price.

The principle is that the chairman of the target company has a legal obligation to act in the best interests of the stockholders. Of course, in reality, the chairman of the corporation is going to act in the best interests of the chairman of the corporation. However, at least he must present the outward appearance of acting in the best interests of the stockholders, whether he really is or not.

The question you will have to ask yourself and keep asking yourself all the time is to what extent the target company is prepared to negotiate in good faith. Probably, they will pretend to negotiate. They will also ask you for a stand-still agreement while the negotiations are going on. This agreement means that you agree not to buy any more stock while the negotiations continue. In the movie *Other People's Money*, they do in fact reach a stand-still agreement, and then both sides rush out and try to buy secretly as much stock as they can in violation of that agreement. In real life, unless you have a particular reason for doing so, you have no reason for standing still. Nevertheless, if your opponent demands a meeting to discuss a stand-still agreement, you have no reason not to want to meet with him. Otherwise, later on, he will tell the judge that you refused to discuss a stand-still agreement with him.

Corporations which are targets of a take-over attempt might do anything. It is impossible to predict their reaction. They might capitulate and give in. Indeed, this probably happens more frequently than those cases where the target corporation decides to fight to the bitter end.

A common tactic is that the management of the target company will vote themselves a 'golden parachute'. In many cases, the management of the target company is only interested in one thing: getting some money for themselves. They will vote themselves a long-term employment contract at a high salary, for example. They will vote themselves severance pay and other benefits. Their primary objective will be to get as much money out of the company treasury and into their pockets before the take-over goes through.

You will probably find it necessary to adopt a realistic approach. If you want management of the target company to give up quickly and allow you to take over, you will probably have no other choice but to allow them to loot the corporate treasury to a certain extent.

It is unfortunate that the Delaware courts have allowed this practice. These 'golden parachutes' have consistently been upheld. This is clearly a morally repugnant practice. It causes the stockholders to lose considerable benefit from the corporation.

There are other things which a corporation can do to stop a take-over. For one, they can amend their by-laws to stagger the terms of the board of directors. The purpose of this is that once the take-over attempt is successful, the new owners of the corporate stock will have to wait for some years before electing a new slate of directors.

However, the corporate raider generally considers this not to be a problem. He assumes that once he has a majority of the outstanding shares, the opposing directors will resign immediately rather than face a lawsuit. The cases where the opposing directors will fight it out to the bitter end are quite rare, but they do happen.

The two basic methods for taking over a corporation are the tender offer and the proxy fight. A proxy fight involves an election similar to an election to a political office. The established management puts up their slate of directors and the insurgent group puts up an opposing slate. Both sides publish ads in the newspapers, stating that the members of their proposed boards are the pillars of their community, whereas the opposing slate consists of a bunch of crooks and criminals whose nefarious activities are beneath contempt. Both sides will try as best they can to obtain photographs of a member of the opposing slate of candidates in bed with a woman other than his wife. Such photographs are supposed to prove that such a person is incapable of running a public company. If you decide to conduct a proxy fight, the other side might send you girls in order to try to achieve this purpose (or boys if they think that you are so inclined).

Proxy fights have one significant advantage. The insurgent group does not need to spend its money buying up shares in the market. Instead, it sends mailings to the stockholders and asks for their vote. The rules of the S.E.C. require the target company to allow these mailings.

However, proxy fights are not really favored. The reason for this is that they generally are a losing proposition. It hardly ever happens that entrenched management is ousted as the result of a proxy fight. In fact, up until about ten or fifteen years ago, it never happened at all. The management had such a tremendous advantage in a proxy fight that any outside group attempting a take over was just wasting its money.

However, the S.E.C. changed its rules in such a way as to make proxy fights feasible. Nowadays, it does occasionally happen that an outside group wins a proxy fight.

The tender offer is the better idea. A tender offer is an offer to all stockholders to purchase their shares. Tender offers require a lot of money. However, they have one big advantage. Tender offers usually succeed. A tender offer usually ends with the entrenched management being ousted and a new group taking over.

There are many other advantages to a tender offer. One is that it goes quicker. The S.E.C. rule is that a tender offer must remain open for a duration of a minimum of twenty business days. However, some tender offers do not even last that long, because established management capitulates before that. A person or group making a tender offer can be sitting in the president's chair twenty business days after the announcement of the commencement of the offer.

Often, the take-over of a public company occurs in stages. First, 5% of the shares are accumulated through purchases in the open market. Then, there is a tender offer. After that, there is a proxy fight. This is quite common. That was the scenario in the movie *Other People's Money*. Again, the movie was entirely realistic on most points.

A question which might be asked is: Why make a tender offer? Why not simply purchase the shares in the open market?

The answer is that usually it is difficult to purchase a majority of the outstanding shares of stock in the open market without disturbing the price. In the example already given, you might be able to buy 5% of the shares at 10 1/8, but you will almost never be able to buy 51% of the shares at that price. The reason is that many of the stockholders will be long term investors. They will have bought the stock thinking about what the price will be five years from now. They will have no intention of selling before that. If the stock price rises to 15 or 20, they still will not think about selling.

However, a tender offer puts them on the spot. They have exactly twenty business days to decide whether to keep their stock or not. If they do not tender their shares, they may lose an opportunity which will never come again. Usually, when a tender offer is made, the bidder pays a significant premium over the last trading price. Sometimes, at the conclusion of a successful tender offer, there are so few remaining shares held by the public other than the bidder that trading stops and the market vanishes. In other words, a stockholder who does not tender his shares may discover that his shares have no market value at all if he does not tender.

A tender offer also puts the target company on the spot. Management of the target company is **required by law** to allow the bidder to conduct mailings to its stockholders. The target company must also make a recommendation to the stockholders whether to accept the tender or not. Naturally, the management of the target company will be hoping that the tender offer will be a failure because they want to keep their own jobs. However, if they tell their stockholders not to tender, then they could be sued by the stockholders for self-dealing. Often, entrenched management of the target company will decide that the safest course is to remain neutral and make no recommendation, even if they are privately opposed to the offer.

This explains the prior statement that the tender offer rules allow the bidder to shoot a big target with a small gun. The only real requirement for making a tender offer is to pay the S.E.C. filing fee, which is one-fiftieth of one per cent of the value of the shares sought to be purchased via the tender offer. In other words, if a bid is made for stock worth $300,000,000 (three hundred million dollars), the S.E.C. filing fee will be $60,000. Of course, $60,000 is beyond the range of the average pocket book, but anyone intending to buy three hundred million dollars worth of stock had better be prepared to spend some money.

Anyone making a tender offer must provide a financial guarantee that he is prepared to pay the money or issue the junk bonds as the case may be. However, he is not required to put up the money in advance.

There are many other advantages to making a tender offer as opposed to trying to buy the stock in the open market. One important advantage is that one is allowed to impose conditions on the offer. For example, one might impose the condition that the offer will be concluded only if at least 51% of the total outstanding shares are tendered. A second condition might be imposed that the bidder will purchase and pay for not more than 52% of the total outstanding shares.

A problem would arise with such an offer if, for example, 60% of the total outstanding shares were tendered. If that happened, a stockholder who tendered 100 shares would receive payment for 87 of his shares and have 13 shares returned. The total number of stockholders of the target corporation would not be reduced.

This would cause a major problem for you later on, especially if you succeed in taking over the target company. As the would-be president of the target corporation, you have to think about what this company will be like after you take over. All of these investors, each still holding 13 shares after your take-over, will be a continuous headache for you. You will have to send them annual reports and proxy statements, at considerable expense both in terms of printing and postage. The average publicly held corporation spends more than $20 per year per stockholder in printing and postage for these annual reports and proxy statements. This adds up to a lot of money. In addition, later on, one of these 13 share stockholders might decide to bring a lawsuit against your corporation. This is only the beginning of a long list of problems associated with having a large number of small stockholders.

The way to avoid this problem would be to have a round up provision in your tender offer materials. This provision would provide that after pro-rationing, any stockholder left with an odd lot would have the number of shares accepted rounded up to the the nearest 100, or the number of shares returned and not accepted rounded down to the nearest 100. However, you would presumably not be allowed to reduce the number of shares accepted from the other tendering stockholders to offset the effect of these shares being rounded up or down.

S.E.C. Rule 14d-8 deals with fractional shares. It states that when a tender is made for less than the total outstanding shares, and more than the number of shares tendered for are received, the securities taken up and paid for should be taken up and paid for pro rata, disregarding fractions. In other words, in the above situation, where you bid for a maximum of 52% of the total outstanding shares, and 60% of the shares are tendered, you are required by S.E.C. rules to accept and pay for the shares 'pro rata, disregarding fractions.' If you are not clear in your instructions to the transfer agent, you might even find that fractional shares have been issued to the tendering stockholders.

The basic principle to be applied in all such situations is that you can do just about anything, provided that you disclose it in advance to the tendering stockholders. The principle upon which federal securities law is based is **full disclosure**. As far as the federal law (as opposed to the state law) is concerned, almost any deal is legal as long as it is disclosed to the affected stockholders and to the S.E.C. either before or after the actions have taken place, in accordance with the various time limits set by law.

To cite an extreme example of this, a number of years ago, I was approached by the president of a small (very small) public company which owned a chain of restaurants in the Miami area. The president wanted to reduce his shareholder servicing costs by buying out all of his odd-lot stockholders. However, he had no money at all. Therefore, he proposed that he would offer to each odd-lot stockholder who tendered all of his shares a dinner for two in his restaurant.

At that time, the stock in his company was trading at about 10 cents per share. This means that a stockholder owning 50 shares had $5.00 worth of stock. However, if the stockholder tried to sell those shares, he would get nothing at all, because the brokerage commissions would eat up the entire proceeds of the sale. Therefore, the stockholder would be better off taking a meal at the restaurant, rather than continuing to hang on to the shares. At the same time, this would be a good form of advertisement for the restaurant owner, who could hope for repeat business.

One interesting feature of this proposal was that each odd lot stockholder who tendered all of his shares would get the dinner for two, regardless of how many shares that he owned. In other words, a stockholder with only one share would receive the same as a stockholder with 99 shares. This might seem unfair, but there was a good reason for it. The purpose of such a tender offer was to reduce the number of stockholders. It costs the same amount to service a holder of 99 shares as it costs to service a holder of one share. Also, the shares were essentially worthless anyway. Therefore, it made logical sense to give the same consideration to each stockholder of record, as long as he tendered all of his shares.

There is a specific rule of the S.E.C. which allows odd-lot stockholders to be given special consideration over the other stockholders. Rule 13e-4 (f)(3)(ii) allows the bidder to accept all shares tendered which are less than 100 shares 'by lot'. That was the provision which made such a tender offer legal.

In spite of these considerations, I was still not entirely sure whether this tender offer would be legal or not. In my opinion, the proposed transaction was legal, as long as full disclosure was made. The restaurant owner apparently had quite a good restaurant. He brought along with him several newspaper articles where his restaurant had received favorable reviews in the Miami area. He proposed to send out these reviews along with his tender offer materials.

In the end, I never wrote the tender offer materials, because he also wanted to pay my fees with a bunch of meals in his restaurant. We even discussed some sort of barter arrangement, without success. Nevertheless, I was so intrigued by his idea that I gave him photocopies of my previous tender offer filings with the S.E.C. free of charge.

I was later told that he did, in fact, use the photocopies I gave him and he did file a tender offer with the S.E.C. However, the tender offer itself turned out to be a flop. Not many of his stockholders were willing to hand in their shares in exchange for a dinner for two in a restaurant in the Miami area.

This is intended to be an example of the principle of full disclosure. Almost every deal is legal from the point of view of the S.E.C., as long as the full facts are disclosed to the investors and to the S.E.C.

Chapter Twelve

Setting the Right Terms

When deciding to make a tender offer, you must make decisions about the terms and conditions of the offer. Remember, your purpose is not to become a big shot. Rather, you want to get the best deal you can for yourself, while also satisfying the stockholders.

Some of the stupidest decisions in all of corporate human history have been made in recent years in connection with tender offers. For example, junk bonds have been issued under conditions where it was clear from the beginning that it would be utterly impossible to service the debt. The most famous beneficiary of this situation was Michael Milken, who received a regular salary of $500,000,000 (five hundred million dollars) per year for putting together junk bond deals. It was an over-reaction to this situation which caused Milken to be sentenced to 10 years in jail, although it is doubtful whether he really did anything which was demonstrably illegal.

The point which must be made here is that the purpose of making a tender offer is to acquire a viable company at an attractive price. The corporate values must be there. Just going out and buying something for the sake of buying it can never be a sound business practice.

We have already used the example of Apple Computer. They have a wonderful product, the Apple Macintosh, but, nevertheless, it is obvious that the market valuation of

$845,000,000 for the stock is too high. Somebody might make a bid to take over this company under the 'greater fool' theory. That is the well established theory which holds that regardless of how big a fool one might be to buy a company, there will always be a greater fool who will pay even more for the same company.

The greater fool theory has stood the test of time and has never been refuted. Nevertheless, a real businessman does not count on the possibility of coming across an even greater fool than he. A real businessman buys real values.

There are plenty of stocks in the market with real values. To take one example, the printing and publishing business in Japan is right now booming. As a result, there is a tremendous shortage of heavy duty presses. Every printing press in Japan is already running at full speed for 24 hours a day. A fancy new Heidelberg machine costs too much money. Therefore, Japanese buyers are going to America in search of older, cheaper machines.

In America, the printing business is bad. Many companies are for sale or are going out of business. Usually, old printing presses are given a low valuation for inventory purposes. Therefore, a Japanese company could take over an American company with a large number of old Heidelberg printing presses and get them essentially for free.

This is just one of many examples. There are countless companies where the assets in the hands of the right buyer would be worth far more than the cost of the stock.

However, the question here is how much should be paid for the stock.

This is a difficult question, with no exact answer. Let us

say, for example, that a stock is trading at $25 per share. We will say that over the last five years, this company has traded as high as $50 per share and as low as $20 per share. After a study of the trading patterns and history of the company, we conclude that most stockholders purchased their shares at an average of $40 per share.

Most stock market investors want to sell at a profit. Therefore, we might conclude that if we bid $35 per share, few investors will accept our tender offer. However, if we bid $45 per share, many, perhaps a majority, will tender their shares.

On the other hand, if we bid $60 per share, we might get 85% of the total outstanding shares.

The question is: What do we want?

If we just want working control of the company, we might decide that all we really want is 51% of the total outstanding shares. In this case, we might decide to bid $42 per share. We also might decide to bid only $30 per share, knowing that we probably will not get more than 20% of the total outstanding shares, but that this 20% might be enough to take over the company after a proxy fight.

If, on the other hand, we want the company because we want the printing presses, we might decide to get it over with and bid $75 per share, figuring that in that case we will get 90% of the total outstanding shares.

What we probably should do first is test the waters with a low bid. Bid only $30 per share, and see what happens.

If we want to spook the company, like I want to spook Sovran Bank, we make a tender offer to buy at $5 per share payable in junk bonds, even though the stock is trading at $10 per share.

There are also all kinds of illegal things which can be done in connection with tender offers. The S.E.C. is on the lookout for these but can never catch all of them.

Let us say, for example, that the target company is trading at $25 per share. Two other companies illegally form a group. One quietly buys 100,000 shares at $25 per share. Then, the other announces a tender offer at $50 per share. The market in the target company then rises to $45 per share.

Why $45 per share? The reason is that the deal is not certain. Many tender offers fall through. The bidder is prohibited by law from paying for the stock prior to the expiration date. Therefore, a stockholder is at risk.

At this point, certain brokers step into the middle to do what is known as 'risk arbitrage'. Brokers like Ivan Boesky before he went to jail would buy at $45 per share in order to sell at $50. If the deal went through, they would make five points of easy profit.

What if the deal did not go through? Ah, there's the rub. Usually, if a deal like this collapses, the stock falls to a price lower that it was prior to the announcement of the tender offer.

Knowing this, the broker who purchased at $25 per share now sells his 100,000 shares to the risk arbitrager at $45 per share, thereby making a profit of $2,000,000. In addition, the same broker sells short another 100,000 shares to another arbitrager, also at $45 per share.

At this point, the second party suddenly decides to withdraw his tender offer. The stock collapses to $20 per share. The broker who sold short 100,000 shares at $45 per share covers his short at $20, and thereby makes a profit of

$2,500,000. Total profit on this transaction: $4,500,000.

What has just been described is a highly illegal scheme which would definitely result in jail time if detected. The S.E.C. does actually catch cases like this and prosecute the people involved. However, for every one case which is caught, there are probably many more which go unapprehended.

The reason for mentioning such a highly illegal scheme in this book is that one must always be alert to these possibilities. The truth is that somebody might do something like that once, twice or even three times and get away with it. However, eventually, even if the scheme is never apprehended by the S.E.C., the free market forces will deal such a scheme a resounding blow.

Corporate managers may know how to run their businesses, but most of them are definitely out of their league when they get involved in games like this. Many of them have not even been through the basic training of working their way through college by playing poker. They should stick to the business they know, rather than risking the stockholder's money in an unsound tender offer.

Tender offers have been around for a long time. They were here long before there were S.E.C. rules to regulate them. However, a few years ago, they suddenly became all the rage. Everybody was running around trying to take over everybody else's business, at all kinds of ridiculous prices. For example, a stock might have a book value of $10 and be trading at $25, with a price/earnings ratio of 10:1. Then, somebody would announce a tender offer to take over that company at $50. Why? Nobody could imagine. However, one of the tried and true theories would always be at work. An even greater fool would come along and bid $60 per share for the same company. The bidding war would escalate. Supposedly, everyone would make money.

Why doesn't that happen any more? The reason is that most of these deals were stupid. One plus one will never equal three, no matter how many times you keep adding them.

The stock market goes through cycles like this. For a few years, new issues are hot and everyone wants to go public. Then, new issues fall out of favor. Everybody wants to go private and buy back the stock they issued to the public. For a period of time, there are conglomerates, and everybody wants to merge. When those mergers start to go bad, everybody wants to divest. Companies start 'spinning-off' their divisions, creating instant new issues of stock.

One sees that one year, every woman wears a long dress, and the next year they all wear short skirts. Stock market managers should be capable of more independent thought than that.

Any stock deal of any kind should be based upon sound underlying values. There are plenty of companies in the market with undervalued stock. However, when tender offers go through a fashionable phase, those companies with real values are neglected. It is always those companies whose stock is too high already that becomes the target for a take-over.

Arguably, the greatest book ever written about stock market dealings is called *Reminiscences of a Stock Operator*. This is a fictional-real book about the life Jesse Livermore, better known as *The Wolf of Wall Street*.

Jesse Livermore started in the stock market as a small child, who never bothered with school. He got a job as a 'qoute boy' in a stock brokerage office in about 1880, reading quotes out loud as they came off of an old fashioned ticker. He would then write the latest prices on a blackboard, so that the assembled men could see. After a few years of this, he found that certain trading patterns became familiar. By knowing what the latest trades were, he found that he could predict, with a high degree of accuracy, what the next trade would be.

At that time, 'bucket shops' were legal. These bucket shops were essentially gambling casinos, where bets were made on the next stock price. The young Jesse Livermore had a small advantage in these gambling casinos. He already knew what the next stock price would be. Before long, Jesse Livermore could walk into any bucket shop and, within a few days, bankrupt the entire shop.

By the time that he was 16 years old, Jesse Livermore had to leave the small town where he lived, because nobody would do business with him. He thereafter toured America. He would come into a small town where nobody knew him, somewhat the way that Paul Newmann would walk into a small pool parlor in the movie *The Hustler*. The town would have to be big enough so that there would be at least three bucket shops that he could play off, one against the others, prolonging his stay in that town for a while.

Naturally, seeing a fresh-faced kid right off the street and not even old enough to shave, the bucket shop operator would assume that he had an easy mark. How could he have known that he was dealing with a seasoned professional, someone who already had ten years experience in the securities business?

Within two weeks, every bucket shop in town would be insolvent and Jesse Livermore would be told by the local authorities to move on. After several years of this, he had exhausted and cleaned out all of the small towns in America like St. Louis, so there was no place left for him to go but to Wall Street itself. New York City was the only place in America with a stock market big enough for him.

Before long, they were on to him on Wall Street as well. One move from Jesse Livermore would be enough to send the stock market crashing. There were always rumors circulating about what Jesse Livermore might be doing. He had to disguise himself, operating under various aliases. Even his book was written under a false name, although there was only one person in America who could possibly have written it.

Jesse Livermore repeatedly faced the mathematical problem of gambler's ruin. He would gamble big and win, which would drive him to gamble even bigger. He did not lose often, but when he lost, he lost everything. Here was a man who could have a net worth of ten million dollars on one day, and then be insolvent to the extent of ten million dollars on the next. This was back in the old days, when ten million dollars was still a lot of money.

His book, *Reminiscences of a Stock Operator*, was written in about 1906 when Jesse Livermore was going through one of his bankruptcy phases and desperately needed money. The book makes it sound like his career was already finished. In fact, however, he not only got himself back on his feet again but, by 1929, he was reputed to be the richest man in America. He had made so much money by his stock market dealings, that it had become completely impossible for him to lose all of it and become insolvent again.

What did Jesse Livermore then do? He solved this problem by jumping out of a window and killing himself. He died without children. This happened in 1929, when the stock market was at its all-time peak. From this incident, sprang the great legend of stock brokers jumping out of windows in 1929.

Within weeks, the stock market itself also crashed. There are old-timers around who still remember this. They claim that it was Jesse Livermore jumping out of that window which caused the world-wide economic depression starting in 1929.

What is the relevance of that story to this book? The answer is that if you try to play the tender offers game, you will be doing something very similar to the kind of thing which Jesse Livermore did. The difference is that he knew what he was doing. You don't. He had been doing this since he was six years old. Do you understand the significance of that? Jesse Livermore may have habitually gambled over his head, but he ultimately succeeded because he knew everything that there was to know about the stock market.

By the way, one reason that I like his book so much is that it also turns out that one of the great stock market operators in that time was a man by the name of Sam Sloan. 'Old Sam Sloan wouldn't take any gruff from anybody', the book says. Sam Sloan earlier also had become one of the richest men in

America, with a net worth approaching one hundred million dollars, and was the President of the Erie Lackawanna Railroad by around the year 1890. Sam Sloan was also one of the founders of what became Citibank and his name is inscribed on the wall at the entrance to their headquarters on Wall Street. There is a statue erected to him in Hoboken, New Jersey. The life of Sam Sloan is recounted in the *History of the Great American Fortunes* as one of the group of the handful of men who completely controlled United States of America behind the scenes, a man who would issue the orders for the President of the United States to follow.

I have never been able to determine conclusively whether I am a blood relative of that Sam Sloan, but I believe that I probably am. Not only do we both have the same name, but we both were Irish Protestants from the same region of Northern Ireland and our ancestors both came from the old country to Philadelphia.

After Jesse Livermore jumped out of that window in 1929, Congress passed the Securities Act of 1933, which specifically made bucket shops illegal. However, Jesse Livermore, in his heyday, had already bankrupted all of them anyway. This is an example of the free market forces working better than any government imposed system of securities regulation.

The major point is this: If you want to get involved in a tender offer, pick a stock with underlying value. Do not assume that you can outsmart the other guy. Assume that he is smarter and more devious than you. Do not pay such a high price for the stock that the company is simply not worth that much. If you really only want to buy 51% of the stock, try to calculate the lowest possible price which will net you that amount. Remember that once you have made a tender offer, you can always raise the price upon ten business days notice, but that it will be difficult for you to lower the price. Try to find out the cost basis for the stock held by a majority of the present stockholders. Remember that most investors are extremely reluctant to sell at a loss. If you know how much a majority of the investors paid for their stock, then bid a little more, but don't get carried away with the irrepressible urge to give away your money.

Chapter Thirteen

The Conflict of Laws

One of the first things to know about tender offers concerns the federal system of government which exists in the United States and almost nowhere else. In America, there are two independent systems of government: The states and the federal government.

The President of the United States does not have the right to call up the Governor of the State of Delaware and tell him what to do. In most other countries of the world, this situation is inconceivable.

State securities laws are generally known as 'blue sky' laws. The old story about this is concerns a case of stock fraud which was tried before a judge. The defendant, a seller of securities, was trying to claim that his securities were a good investment. At some point, the judge countered, 'What you are trying to do here is you are trying to sell the blue in the sky.'

That decision also explains the difference between the state and federal laws. As far as the S.E.C. is concerned, you are perfectly welcome to sell the blue in the sky to your investors, as long as you fully disclose to them that the blue is what they are buying, and disclose the quality of the air and so on.

However, certain, but not all, states are merit states. In California, for example, in order to convince the Commissioner of Corporations to allow your shares to be sold in that state, you must convince him that your stock makes a good investment. This would be virtually impossible to do in the case of a new and untried company.

In the field of tender offers, you are trying to buy securities, not to sell them. You may run into the problem that certain states have anti-takeover laws. Most of these states are in the Pacific Northwest. A state like Idaho, for example, might have a law which prohibits a corporation located in another state from taking over any corporation headquartered in Idaho.

The state will claim that they have the need to do this to protect the jobs of Idaho workers. If a corporation headquartered in Idaho is taken over by a Miami corporation and moved to Florida, the reasoning is that the industry of Idaho will suffer.

However, the general opinion in other states is that this violates the commerce clause of the Constitution of the United States. That is the clause which prohibits one state from imposing tariffs and import duties on products from other states.

The resulting situation forms part of a field known as 'conflict of laws'. There have been many decisions of the United States Supreme Court on this. In general, the states are losing the battle. Still, prior to making a tender offer, the state laws must be checked. The best place to get this information would be the *Commerce Clearing House Blue Sky Law Reporter*, which is available in many law libraries. On the other hand, there is probably not a single copy of that publication in Japan. A telephone call to the commissioner of securities in the state of the target corporation might be the quickest way to obtain a copy of the pertinent state securities laws.

After the state securities commissioner has informed you that your proposed tender offer is absolutely illegal under the laws of his state and that he is prepared to issue a stop order against it, you will have to decide what to do. You might decide to look for another target corporation. However, the state securities commissioner probably does not have the power to enforce his stop orders outside of that particular state. If you are bold enough, you might decide simply to ignore him.

This problem will probably not arise because your target corporation is, more likely than not, incorporated either in New York or in Delaware. Neither of these two states has an anti-takeover law.

Once you feel that you have thoroughly researched the law, and/or if you feel courageous enough to step into unchartered waters, it is time to announce your tender offer. However, prior to taking this bold step, you need to reassess your situation.

It must be borne in mind that this is a serious game that you are playing. You have to have nerves of steel. You must assume that there is a high probability of your being sued. You can expect to be sued by your target corporation. You also have to anticipate the possibility of being sued by the S.E.C. This is serious business. You might wind up spending years in court. Just bear in mind that you will be trying to take away a corporation from somebody who feels that it belongs to him. You cannot expect smooth sailing. Among other things, you should have an attorney lined up to represent you when (not if) you wind up in federal court over this.

Before doing this, you might consider looking up the Texaco-Pennzoil Case. In that case, in the Texas courts, the losing side had to pay the winning side one billion dollars in triple damages. For you to have to pay one billion dollars might put a serious dent in even **your** life style. Just don't go jumping out of windows over this.

If you really believe that you have the fortitude to join the ranks of T. Boone Pickens, Ivan Boesky, Carl Ichan and the ghost of Robert Maxwell, proceed forward. However, not many people are prepared to wage the outright war that will probably be necessary for your tender offer to be successful.

Remember that there is nothing worse than to go half-way and get involved in a deal like this and then to realize that you don't have the stomach for it and back out.

Having thought and re-thought about this, and having decided that you are still willing to go forward, it is time to proceed.

The first step is a public announcement of your tender offer. There are many ways to do this. The simplest is to write a letter to the target corporation and issue a press release. The preferred method is a newspaper advertisement in the *Wall Street Journal* or in another national newspaper such as the *Investors Business Daily*. This is covered by S.E.C. Rule 14d-4.

There are two types of newspaper advertisements. These are called the 'long form' and the 'summary publication'. The long form consists of almost the entire offering circular being printed in the newspaper. A half-page ad in the Wall Street Journal would not be uncommon for this purpose.

The summary publication is somewhat shorter. You give the basic facts plus your name and address to which the stockholders can write for the complete tender offer materials, plus your telephone number.

Ads in the Wall Street Journal are not cheap. It will be difficult for you to get away with an ad costing less than $10,000. Therefore, you might want to try a cheaper publication. However, S.E.C. Rule 14d-4(b) states that 'adequate publication of a tender offer pursuant to this section may require publication in a newspaper with a national circulation'.

Note the words 'may require'. Like so many S.E.C. rules, they are vague on details. If all of the stockholders happen to live in Richmond, Virginia, the publication of an ad in the *Richmond Times Dispatch* might be good enough, but that will rarely be the case.

Is the *Los Angeles Times* a newspaper of national circulation? What about the *Amsterdam News*, a newspaper published in Harlem, but read by members of a certain racial minority all across America?

Another way to announce your tender offer is to conduct a mailing to all of the stockholders. This is the most effective means of all. However, you can only get the stockholder's list if the target corporation is willing to give it to you. If you are on friendly terms with them, they will be willing to give you the list. However, if this is to be a hostile tender offer, they will resist giving you the list.

At about this time, you might feel that this is the time to contact the S.E.C. The telephone number of their Office of Tender Offers is (202) 272-3097. This office is located only in the headquarters of the S.E.C. in Washington, D.C. The S.E.C. branch offices in various cities around the United States have no authority when it comes to tender offers.

Dealing with the S.E.C. is dangerous and tricky business. To begin with, the S.E.C. will be careful to tell you that they cannot tell you what to do. Then, having said that, they will tell you what to do.

Throughout this tender offer, the S.E.C. should remain invisible to the public. You should never tell anybody that you spoke to the S.E.C. and that this is what they told you to do. Rather, you will say that you did this because you felt that your actions were morally and legally correct, never because the S.E.C. made you do it.

Otherwise, the S.E.C. will get angry at you quickly. There is nothing worse than being a target of the S.E.C. If you think that you read something in the Constitution of the United States about Freedom of Speech, just forget about that.

One thing which you should absolutely never ever do is say to anybody words like: 'The S.E.C. has approved this deal,' or 'We cleared it with the S.E.C.' I realize that people say things like this all the time. However, those who do this are courting danger.

Similarly, things which you should never say to anybody at all are words such as: 'I really like the S.E.C. The S.E.C. has a fine staff. They are a group of wonderful people. There is no organization in America better than the S.E.C. I support fully all of their administrative decisions.'

Say nothing like that. Do not under any circumstances ever say anything at all, good or bad, about the S.E.C. That is the only safe course.

Remember that you didn't hear it from me.

Why is the S.E.C. so concerned about this? Actually they have a good reason. Every day, investors call the S.E.C. and say something like this: 'I bought stock in XYZ Corporation and the stock went down. I lost money. I demand that you investigate this. They can't be allowed to get away with it. How could you possibly approve of such a thing?'

The maker of such a telephone call is almost always a woman. When such a call comes in, the receptionist politely informs the caller that this was not approved by the S.E.C., because the S.E.C. never approves or disapproves of anything at all.

After you have announced your tender offer, usually with an ad in the *Wall Street Journal*, you then must promptly file what is known as a Schedule 14D-1 with the S.E.C. This Schedule 14D-1 will contain as exhibits your offer to purchase and your letter of transmittal.

Perhaps the most difficult job which you will do in connection with this entire tender offer will be to prepare this Schedule 14D-1. You can find a copy of the form on pages 208-215 of your handy volume of *Code of Federal Regulations, Vol. 17, Part 240 to End.* You should have prepared your Schedule 14D-1 in advance and have it ready for filing on the same day that you announce your tender offer. Otherwise, it might take weeks to prepare this document and you will be in serious trouble with the S.E.C.

Schedule 14D-1 is a disclosure document. It is supposed to contain all of the information which an investor needs to know to make an informed decision as to whether to accept your tender offer or not. You will need to disclose everything about yourself and everything which you know about the target company. The types of questions which must be answered by this form are the name, address, telephone number and citizenship of the bidder. However, it goes far beyond that. The balance sheet of the bidder must be disclosed. Also, the future plans for the target corporation if the tender offer is successful must be disclosed.

This last point is important. The worst thing which you can possibly do is not reveal some vital piece of information in the offer to purchase. If you say that you plan to do one thing, and later on make no effort to do that but instead do something else, you could be in serious trouble. At the same time, there is no good reason not to tell the truth initially. Nobody except your opponent reads these documents anyway, so if you reveal some horrible secret about yourself and about your long career as a child molester, it will cause no harm. Therefore, if your tender offer involves the issuance of junk bonds, be sure to state clearly in your offer to purchase that these bonds are strictly junk. Only if you fail to disclose something will you get into trouble with the S.E.C.

Why must the balance sheet of the bidder be disclosed? The reason among others is that the stockholders need to be able to make the determination as to whether you have the money to pay for the stock or not.

This is an important point. In order to make a tender offer, you do not need to be able to put up the money in advance. However, you need to show a capability of paying for the stock. There are many ways to achieve this. One way is this: Go to a bank with which you have an established relationship. Get them to guarantee to loan you the money to pay for all shares validly tendered. This commitment must be in writing. Then file this commitment with the S.E.C. as an exhibit to your Schedule 14D-1. In addition, you must include the balance sheet of the bank to show that they have the money to pay for the stock.

In every tender offer, there are standard clauses for conditions. For example, you might state in your tender offer that you reserve the right to withdraw the offer in the case of war, famine, civil unrest, in case the target corporation files for bankruptcy and so on. At the same time, you must make a firm commitment that in case those things do not happen, you will buy and pay for the stock.

The following is a standard clause which might be found in a typical tender offer. (This happens to be one I wrote myself although, as usual, I copied it from somebody else):

> **13. Certain conditions of the offer.** Notwithstanding any other provision of the offer (a) the Purchaser may terminate or amend the offer as to any shares not then accepted for payment, shall not be required to accept for payment or to pay for any shares or may delay the acceptance of payment for shares tendered if at any time prior to the acceptance for payment of such shares there shall have occurred (1) any material adverse change in the company's financial condition, assets, business or operations subsequent to the date of the offer or, (2) the Company shall have authorized, recommended, proposed or publicly announced its intention to enter into tender or exchange offer, merger, consolidation,

liquidation, dissolution, business combination, recapitalization, acquisition or disposition of a material amount of assets other than in the ordinary course of business.

The foregoing conditions are for the sole benefit of the Purchaser and may be asserted or waived by the purchaser in whole or in part at any time or from time to time in its discretion.

The first step is to obtain copies of tender offers which other people have filed in the recent past. You then study and copy them. You should obtain at least five or ten samples. Naturally, you will try to find tender offers similar to yours.

The way to do this is to contact a company called Disclosure, Inc. They are headquartered at 5161 River Road, Bathesda, Maryland 20816 but have branch offices in all of the major cities. Their mailing address is: Disclosure, P.O. Box 64352, Baltimore, MD 21264-4352. Their telephone number is (301) 951-1455. In Washington, D.C., you can contact them at (202) 347-2824. You call them and establish an account with them. You tell them that you want all recent Schedule 14D-1 filings of a certain type. They will charge you an hourly rate to search for these documents on their computer. These documents will be stored on their compact disk. They have the most advanced and up-to-date equipment. In a matter of seconds, they can print from their compact disk a hard paper copy of anything that you want which has ever been filed with the S.E.C.

They do not charge by the page. Rather, they charge by

the document. If you want a Schedule 14D-1, you have to pay $35. It doesn't matter whether the Schedule 14D-1 is 20 pages long or 200 pages long, you still have to pay the same amount.

Don't complain about this. This is really quite a bargain. The person who prepared that 14D-1 may easily have paid $50,000 in lawyer's fees just to prepare that one document. However, you get it for only $35. There is no copyright on such things. These are all public documents. You can just copy his work product.

You will not be the only one doing this. I once filed a tender offer under a new rule of a new and original type, which nobody had ever done before. A few months later, I wanted to do another one, so I ordered copies of the work done in the meantime by others. I got a document filed by Sullivan and Cromwell, perhaps the leading law firm in the securities field. In going through their materials, some of their language seemed familiar. I checked back through my own documents, and I verified what I had suspected: Sullivan and Cromwell had copied word for word some original clauses I had written and filed in my own document with the S.E.C. Also, I knew that they could not have gotten this language from anybody else, because mine had been the first tender offer of this particular type.

In short, Sullivan & Cromwell, knowingly or not, used the legal language copied from Sam Sloan, and no doubt charged their client a $100,000 fee for this.

I must mention here that I have often been the ghost writer for companies filing tender offers. My own name never appears. Undoubtedly, Sullivan & Cromwell never knew that they had copied my work product.

Actually, copying the work of someone else is not only legal, but it is the safest thing to do. Somebody who has already filed a Schedule 14D-1 with the S.E.C. and did not get into trouble has already tested the water. The safest thing to do is simply to copy his example.

Even after you have liberally copied the examples of other people's tender offers, you will find that preparing a Schedule 14D-1 is a tremendously difficult thing to do. It will require a bare minimum of 30-40 hours of work. For this reason, you should have prepared your Schedule 14D-1 prior to the public announcement of your tender offer. Once you have obtained copies of other people's Schedule 14D-1 from Disclosure, perhaps you should have your secretary type them into a word processor, excluding the exhibits. It then becomes a cut and paste operation.

One the exhibits to your Schedule 14D-1 will be your *Offer to Purchase*. This is the document of utmost importance because this is the document which you will be mailing to the stockholders. Another document will be the letter of transmittal. Most letters of transmittal are the same, so you can almost lift directly somebody else's letter of transmittal. However, be sure to copy the Substitute Form W-9 on the back. This is the form used to obtain the Social Security number of the person tendering his shares. You will be required by law to provide this information to the IRS later on. You will also be required by law to prepare a Form 1099 of the IRS and mail it to each tendering stockholder after the end of the current tax year.

Usually, when tender offer materials are mailed out, the envelope also contains a cover letter, a letter to the brokers, a form letter from the broker to the clients, a copy of the latest IRS regulations, and a return reply envelope. I personally tend to feel that this is all junk. When I mail tender offer materials to a stockholder, I want him to read my stuff. The best way to convince him not to read my stuff is to include in the same envelope a bulky copy of some IRS regulations, which the stockholder could easily obtain for himself at the local IRS office, and which almost never applies to the stockholder anyway. However, my opinion is the minority view. Undoubtedly, your lawyer is going to tell you to include the IRS regulations, so that he can charge you a high fee for this advice.

Until this point, I have avoided the subject of lawyers. This is a hot topic. It is virtually impossible to conduct a tender offer without the benefit of a lawyer. In fact, I am the only person who has ever done it, as far as I am aware. However, lawyer fees trend to be on the astronomical side.

To cite one example, there was a recent article in the *New York Times* about a 'small' law firm with less than 100 lawyers which charged $100,000,000 in fees last year only for defending against tender offers. That was more than one million dollars per lawyer per year.

I would be doing a great disservice to the reader if I led him to believe that he could successfully conduct a tender offer without the benefit of a lawyer. Of course, it could be done, but what if the target company files a lawsuit against you?

At the same time, while a lawyer is necessary, it is also necessary to take steps to keep legal costs under control.

This is a serious matter. A lawyer undertaking to represent

a client in a tender offer will expect to be paid a fee starting at $100,000 and going up from there. Obviously, having to pay a fee to a lawyer in the amount of $100,000 will often make a tender offer unattractive.

The best way to try to get around this problem is only to give those tasks to a lawyer which only a lawyer can do.

The one thing which only a lawyer can do is appear in court on behalf of a corporation. Almost any other task can be performed by a non-lawyer. For example, writing a Schedule 14D-1, a letter of transmittal and an offer to purchase is a task which a non-lawyer can do just about as well as a lawyer. What you can do is have someone write the 14D-1 or write it yourself and then give it to the lawyer for proof reading and checking.

Many lawyers will refuse to proceed on this basis. They will want to be in control of the entire deal and do everything themselves.

When that happens, you get another lawyer. It would be suicidal to give all decision making authority in a tender offer over to a lawyer. Would you place your lawyer in charge of your business? Of course not. Why, then, should you place him in charge of your tender offer?

As an example of how your lawyer might get you into trouble, he might tell you that in order to make a tender offer, you must put the funds to pay for the stock in escrow. In fact, there is no such rule. Anybody would have to be crazy to put their funds in escrow in the case of a hostile tender offer. You could be sued by your opponent and the funds could be tied up in litigation for years. However, your lawyer is not concerned about that. He wants your funds to be tied up in litigation for years, so that he can collect his substantial legal fee to fight the court case to get your funds back.

You must remember that there is a natural conflict of interest between yourself and your lawyer. Your objective will be to take over the target corporation as cheaply as possible. Your lawyer's objective will be to generate as much legal fees as possible, and yet still get paid for his services. This creates a problem, but, nevertheless, you will almost certainly not be able to complete a tender offer without the benefit of a lawyer.

Another factor is that there are only a handful of lawyers in the entire United States of America who really know what they are doing in the field of tender offers. One of them is Sullivan and Cromwell, but you do not have enough money to afford them. Most of the qualified law firms who specialize in this area have a fee schedule starting at one million dollars and going up from there.

The question you ask is: Why don't I just walk down the street until I find a storefront which says 'Abogado', and walk in and hire that lawyer.

The answer is that that lawyer will not take your case. The reason is that he needs lawyer's liability insurance in the securities field. No lawyer is going to get involved in a securities case without an insurance policy to protect him, and these insurance policies are expensive. For that reason, only lawyers who are already practicing in the securities field will be prepared to take your case.

This is perhaps the biggest problem you will face in connection with your tender offer. You must have a lawyer and, at the same time, you must keep his costs under control. Your lawyer may not know much, if indeed anything at all, about federal securities law, but you can be sure that he will know how to tell his secretary to type up your monthly bill.

The Schedule 14D-1 which you must file at the commencement of the tender offer is a perfect example of this. The preparation of this document requires a tremendous amount of work. If you give this job to your lawyer, he might easily charge you a fee of $50,000 for this alone. However, any person of moderate intelligence could prepare a Schedule 14D-1, provided only that he has a bunch of examples of other Schedules 14D-1 obtained from Disclosure, Inc.

Your lawyer will not be happy about this, but you should tell him that you will have a clerk in your office write the Schedule 14D-1, but you will give it to the lawyer for his comments and corrections.

You have a right to question everything which your lawyer tells you. Again, most of these lawyers really have no idea of what they are talking about. They will tell you all kinds of ridiculous things, and then get angry when you fail to follow their advice.

Nevertheless, you need a lawyer to complete a tender offer almost as much as you need a woman if you want to produce a child.

If possible, you should try to keep your lawyer in the background. Your opponent will hire a lawyer and then his lawyer will want to know the name of your lawyer in order to know who to talk to. Your answer to that question should be: 'If you want to talk, talk to me'.

Lawyers love to talk to each other, for hours and hours. You call your lawyer and spend one hour talking to him. For that, he charges you a fee of $150. Then, he talks to the opposing lawyer for one hour to tell him what you said. For that, each lawyer charges his own client $150. Then the opposing lawyer talks to his client for one hour. Again, the charge is $150. As a result, the total legal fees for this one item for both sides comes to $600.

After that, the answer from your opponent comes back, through the same process. Again, the total charges come to $600. Thus, you have paid a total of $1200 to communicate with your opponent.

On the other hand, you could have talked directly to your opponent and he could have talked to you for free. No legal charges would have been involved.

My father, who was a lawyer, and who also worked for the IRS, had a favorite story about this. There were two farmers and a cow. The cow wandered from one farmer's field to the other. The one farmer said, 'This is my cow.' The other farmer said, 'No. This is my cow.' Each farmer hired a lawyer. The case was filed in court. The case went on for years and years. The legal fees each side was paying mounted. Finally, both farmers had to give up their farms to pay the lawyer's fees. The two lawyers got the farms, killed the cow, split it up and eat it for dinner.

This is the reason that your lawyer will insist that all negotiations with the other side be conducted through him. This is also the reason that you should resist this demand. You should make it absolutely clear to everyone involved that only you have the authority to negotiate for your side, and that no lawyer has that authority.

Chapter Fourteen

The Letter of Transmittal

One of the documents which you will have to prepare in connection with this tender offer is known as a 'Letter of Transmittal'. This is usually a long sheet of paper which the stockholder attaches to his stock certificate when he sends in his stock. On a tender offer I did recently, I set some sort of record by writing a letter of transmittal which was 14 inches long. Typically, these days, a letter of transmittal is three to four feet long.

The reason for a letter of transmittal is that when the stockholder tenders his shares to you, he is not exactly selling the shares. Rather, he is transmitting the shares to you under certain terms and conditions. When these terms and conditions have been fulfilled, you will send him the money to pay for the stock. If these conditions are not fulfilled, you will return the shares to him.

For this reason, when the stockholder sends in the shares, he does not sign the back of the stock certificate. Instead, he signs the letter of transmittal. He will also take the letter of transmittal to any commercial bank or to any stock broker who is a member of the NASD and get his signature guaranteed. Banks offer this as a service to their customers. Note that a signature guarantee from a savings and loan is not acceptable. It must be from a commercial bank.

Every major stock transfer agent has books on file with

specimen signatures of every authorized signer of almost every commercial bank in the United States. Therefore, in a questionable or disputed case, the stock transfer agent will be able to verify the signatures of the guarantors.

There will always be stockholders who do not follow the instructions you send them and sign the back of the stock certificate instead. There is nothing wrong with this. However, if the deal falls through and you must return the shares, you will have to endorse the shares back to him.

As a general rule, you will want to hire a depositary to receive the tendered shares. The depositary will generally be a bank. The stockholders who tender their shares will mail in the certificates along with the signed letter of transmittal to the depositary. The depositary will check the signatures to see if they have been properly endorsed. He will check for defects or irregularities on the stock certificates. Then, he will keep the shares until the tender offer has been concluded, and, if the deal is successful, he will then hand the shares over to the transfer agent.

For these services, he will charge you a fee. Typically, the fee might be $5,000. You can shop around on this. Preferably, you should hire the same bank which is already acting as the transfer agent for the target company. However, they might refuse your business on the grounds of 'conflict of interest'. If that situation arises, almost every bank in the Wall Street Financial District in New York City will provide this service. My personal preference has always been the U.S. Trust of New York. The fees vary widely from bank to bank. In general, they will charge you a set-up fee, plus a fee for each tender which is received and processed.

Chapter Fifteen

The Response to Your Newspaper Advertisement

After you have announced your tender offer via an ad in the *Wall Street Journal,* the first call you will receive, at exactly 9:00 A.M. on the first day, will be a call from Depository Trust Company. Their telephone number is (212) 709-1449.

They will be calling you for information about your tender offer. They will put this information, including your phone number, into their computer, which will relay that information to virtually every major stock brokerage firm in America. Far more people who are important to you will read that information on their computer screens than will read your name in the *Wall Street Journal.*

Within minutes after receiving your first call from Depository Trust Company, they will enter this information about your tender offer into their computer, and this information will be broadcast around the world. Soon, your telephone will be ringing off the hook. Your telephone will not stop ringing for at least the next twenty business days.

In addition to Depository Trust Company, many other financial information and stock market retrieval services will be calling you for the latest information about your tender offer. One call you will receive will be from Financial Information Inc. They publish the Financial Daily Card Service, among other services, which are subscribed to by most of the stock brokerage firms in America. You will also receive calls from the National Clearing Corporation, from the Independent Election Committee and from various other organizations in the business of providing this sort of financial information to their clients. There will also be clipping services who will clip your ad from the *Wall Street Journal* and provide copies to their customers.

Depository Trust Company will want to set up a 'book entry system' for your tender offer. The reason for this is that most of the shares which will ultimately be tendered through your tender offer will come from Depository Trust Company. They act as the agent for almost every broker which is a member of the New York Stock Exchange.

The way this works is this: A typical customer comes to a Merrill, Lynch branch office with 100 shares of XYZ Corp he wants to put into his account. The Merrill, Lynch branch office sends the shares to the Merrill, Lynch head office. The Merrill, Lynch head office might send the shares to the transfer agent. However, more likely, they will send the shares to Depository Trust Company, also known as 'DTC'. DTC will send the shares to the transfer agent with instructions to transfer the shares into the name of Cede & Co. This is known as a 'nominee name'. The reason for the use of a nominee name is that it is somewhat harder to transfer shares held in the name of a corporation, because corporate resolutions must be attached, which creates possible legal complications. To avoid this, the name of Cede & Co. is used. Cede & Co. is a limited partnership.

After getting the shares back from the transfer agent, DTC

will put them in their vault, along with several billion dollars worth of other securities. From then on, all shares held by DTC become a computer entry. Brokers buy and sell these shares between each other. However, they do not deliver the physical certificates. Instead, they settle the transaction with computer entries through DTC.

At any time, any broker who is a participant with DTC can order physical delivery of the certificates. DTC will instruct the transfer agent to deliver the shares to the broker. All this is done by computer. Usually, the broker takes physical delivery of the shares only when the customer is asking to receive his shares. Otherwise, the broker would prefer to leave his shares with DTC, to eliminate the possibility of the shares being lost or stolen.

DTC is going to play a big role in your tender offer, so you need to know about them. After you make your tender offer, you are going to be required to mail offering materials to the major stock brokers. For example, Merrill, Lynch will inform you of how many of its customers own shares in the target corporation. You must send to the Merrill, Lynch Expirations Department one set of offering materials for each customer they have. Other brokers do not have an expirations department. Instead, they have a reorganization department.

The reorganization department is your best friend. They are required by law to forward your tender offer materials to all of their customers who are holding stock in the target corporation. They must inform them of your tender offer and request from them a decision on whether to tender their shares or not. Finally, the broker must not miss the expiration date, under penalty of law.

The telephone and FAX numbers of some of the major reorganization departments are as follows: Paine, Webber tel. (201) 902-5698; Dean, Witter tel. (212) 392-2101; Smith Barney tel. (212) 356-2805, FAX (212) 356-2076; Kidder Peabody tel. (212) 510-8072, FAX (212) 510-8086; A. G. Edwards FAX (314) 289-7342; Advest Co. tel. (203) 525-1421, FAX (203) 241-2086; Spear, Leeds tel. (212) 587-8838; Lewco Securities tel. (212) 440-9735, FAX (212) 440-9714; Herzog, Heine tel. (212) 908-4288, FAX (212) 908-4265; Legg, Mason tel. (301) 539-3400; Shearson, Lehman tel. (212) 464-1411; National Financial Services tel. (212) 335-5518; Charles Schwab FAX (415) 395-6902; Kemper Clearing FAX (414) 272-1253; John Hancock Clearing FAX (212) 225-8695.

While your tender offer is pending, you are likely to be in contact with the above brokers almost every day.

If it happens that their customer has gone to Timbuktu on vacation, then the broker has to call long distance to the Republic of Mali to ask the customer whether he wants to tender his shares to you or not. This service is performed at essentially no cost to you or to the tendering stockholder. Neither of you has to pay a commission.

Let us say, for example, that Prudential Securities informs you that they have 24 customers who own shares in your target corporation. Then you must send 24 sets of the tender offering materials to the Prudential Securities Reorganization Department. This is required by Rule 14d-5(f)(4)(vi).

Let us say, for example, that later on, 14 customers decide to tender their shares, amounting to 2742 shares in all, and the remaining 10 either decide not to tender or do not make any decision. In that case, the Prudential Securities Reorganization Department will inform DTC that 14 security holders representing 2742 shares, for example, have decided to tender. If that happens, DTC will transfer by computer 2742 shares from the account of the broker to your account, which they will have established for you with DTC.

One of the most important rules regarding tender offers is that any person accepting a tender offer has a right to change his mind and withdraw his shares up until the expiration date and hour. Because of this, you are also prohibited from paying for the shares up until the expiration date. For that reason, DTC will hold the shares in your account with them until the expiration date arrives. When you are ready to pay for the shares, you will wire the funds to the account of DTC at Chemical Bank. DTC will not accept a check in the mail. You must wire the money by federal funds. When sending the funds, you also have to call up Henry Padrone at DTC at (212) 709-1788 and tell him that the funds are on the way. You must give Henry this information by 1:00 P.M., so that he can credit the funds to his customers, which are the brokers, on the same day.

If you ever do call up DTC, every five seconds you will hear a beep on the telephone. This is to warn you that the conversation is being recorded. Dealing with DTC is serious business. They are holding billions of dollars in securities. This is the reason that every telephone conversation is recorded. I hope that no reader of this book, armed with this information, will make frivolous calls to DTC, because they also have equipment which informs them where every telephone call is coming from. If you try to pull some funny business on DTC, they will catch you and put you in jail.

Chapter Sixteen

Contacting the Stockholders

After you have announced your tender offer with the publication of an ad in the *Wall Street Journal*, your telephone will be ringing off the hook every day. You will need to have someone sleeping next to the telephone all hours of the day and night. You will have to answer all kinds of questions.

One way to handle this problem is to hire an agent to perform this service. Shareholder Communications Corporation, 40 Exchange Place, New York, N.Y. 10005 is a specialist in this field. They have a bank of about 100 telephones to receive incoming calls like this. Their major telephone numbers are (212) 809-3600 and 1-800-221-5724. The President of Shareholder Communications Corporation is Al Miller. They have a highly qualified staff consisting primarily of underemployed stage actors, who practice playing the role of a corporate executive answering his telephone.

The services offered by Shareholder Communications Corporation are not cheap. However, they do a job which cannot easily be performed elsewhere. They do more than merely have a person sitting by the telephone all the time. They will also obtain the telephone number of every stockholder of record, call up the stockholder, explain the tender offer to him and ask him to tender his shares. If there are 10,000 stockholders of record, this can be a big job.

This is only the beginning of the services which

Shareholder Communications Corporation will perform. In addition, they will track down and locate every stockholder of record who has moved and left no forwarding address. They have a copy of every telephone directory published in the entire United States of America to help them to find these people. If they cannot find a person, they will locate some relative and ask him where that person is. They will call up everybody with the same last name in the telephone book. Eventually, they find almost everybody, with the exception of those people who are already dead, in which case they attempt to find their heirs.

Experience has shown that a far greater number of stockholders of record will tender their shares after they have received a call from Shareholder Communications Corporation. Their services can be essential to the success of any tender offer.

However, your first priority must be to obtain the use of the stockholder list of the target company. The way that you do this is to send the following letter (This letter is a typical Sam Sloan special, but you are welcome to compose another one):

> Dear Sirs:
>
> ABC Corporation has today announced a tender offer to purchase all of the outstanding common shares of XYZ Corporation at a price of $14 per share, through publication of an advertisement in the national edition of the Wall Street Journal.

This is to advise you that we hereby demand pursuant to Rule 14d-5(e) promulgated under the Securities Exchange Act of 1934 that you provide us with a copy of your stockholders list and security position listings pursuant to Rule 14d-5(a) under that Act for the purpose of disseminating all of the tender offer materials to your stockholders.

This is to further advise you that we are aware of and will comply with the provisions of paragraph (f) of Rule 14d-5. Furthermore, pursuant to subparagraph (a)(1) under that paragraph of that rule, we hereby elect to require your company to disseminate all amendments disclosing all material changes to the tender offer materials pursuant to that section.

The name, address and telephone number of the person to contact pursuant to paragraph (a)(4) of that section is Mohammad Ismail Sloan, President of ABC Corporation, 666 Chicken Street, Kabul, Afghanistan, tel. 666-1998.

Very Truly Yours,

Samuel H. Sloan, President

This letter will force the target corporation to do one of two things. Either they must supply you with their stockholders list or they must agree to mail your tender offer materials to the stockholders at your expense. This is required by Rule 14d-5(c)(1). In addition, S.E.C. Rule 14d-5(a)(4) states that no later than the second business day after the above letter demanding the stockholders list, the subject company must respond orally to your demand. Furthermore, S.E.C. Rule 14d-5(b)(2) states that 'no later than the third business day' after receipt of the above letter, the subject company must commence the mailing of your tender offering materials to their stockholders.

This is one of the most important weapons at your disposal. In fact, without this, it would become difficult successfully to conclude a tender offer.

Almost invariably, the target corporation will decide not to reveal its stockholder list to the bidder but rather will opt to mail the bidder's literature to the stockholders. The target corporation is allowed to bill the bidder for the costs of these services. This is covered by Rule 14d-5(g)(2). Essentially, the costs are to be computed as the costs to mail the last annual report to the stockholders, excluding printing expenses, but plus sufficient postage for a first class mailing. Also, the target corporation may not charge for the cost of employee's time, but may charge for the cost of preparing mailing labels. This is all covered by Rule 14d-5(g)(2)(iv).

It must be mentioned that you are not required to conduct a mailing to the stockholders. If the target corporation is listed on the New York Stock Exchange and its management does not own many shares, it might be possible to conduct a successful tender offer without bothering with a mailing to the stockholders. However, the benefits of a direct mailing are so great and the relative costs are so small, that it would seem foolish not to conduct a stockholder mailing.

After you have conducted your mailing to the stockholders, the target corporation is required to respond. Again, this works to your advantage. The target corporation must file eight copies of a Schedule 14D-9 with the S.E.C. and send one copy to you by hand delivery.

More importantly, the target corporation must, no later than 10 business days after the commencement of your tender offer, mail at its expense a letter to all stockholders of record, which recommends acceptance or rejection of your tender offer, or expresses no opinion and remains neutral, or states that it is unable to take a position with respect to your tender offer, and gives the reasons therefore. This is required by Rule 14e-2(b).

All of this puts the management of the target corporation on the spot. Without this rule, your opponent would probably stonewall, say nothing, and pretend that your offer does not exist. However, because of this rule, he must commit himself one way or the other. Even if he is strenuously opposed to your tender offer, he will probably be reluctant to say so in writing. If he does say so, the stockholders will probably see through his letter and realize that he is acting in his own selfish interests, not in the interests of the stockholders. In short, any response he gives will be of benefit to you.

Chapter Seventeen

Obeying the Rules

Once your tender offer has started, there are any number of possible things which might happen. This is a difficult subject to write about, because absolutely everything is possible. However, here are a few guidelines.

It must be remembered that everything goes according to rules. However, the rules do not cover all possible situations. Every case is different. Rules will be imposed on your tender offer which clearly should not apply. However, the rules must be maintained for the sake of uniformity.

One thing which you should never even think about is disobeying the rules. You must remember that it is only because of these rules that your tender offer has any chance of succeeding. For example, it is under the rules that the target corporation is required to allow you to mail your literature to their stockholders. That rule is of somewhat recent origin. Prior to that rule, there was no snowball's chance of a party making a hostile tender offer having a chance to communicate directly by mail with the shareholders. It was necessary in those times for the bidder to attempt to communicate with the stockholders through newspaper advertisements.

However, it will often happen that there is a legitimate disagreement as to what a rule means. The S.E.C. will call you and tell you that such-and-such rule requires such-and-such action. You then read that rule and can find no such thing.

The S.E.C. also issues interpretations of its rules. These change from time to time. There are also 'staff opinions' which are published in such places as the *Commerce Clearing House Federal Securities Law Reporter*. Every now and then, they publish one of these in response to one of my own inquiries.

An example of how changeable the S.E.C. can be is found in a tender offer in which I was involved in 1981. I had been hired to write the tender offering materials for a small company wanting to buy back the shares from its odd-lot stockholders for the purpose of reducing the stockholder servicing costs. My proposal was that each stockholder would be paid a $25 bonus for tendering all of his shares, regardless of whether he tendered one share or 99 shares. There was a specific provision in the rules under Section 13(e) which allowed this sort of bonus to be paid. This was a standard deal.

However, this particular tender offer had a special twist. In this case, the corporation itself was not exactly buying back its own shares. Instead, the Employee Stock Ownership Plan controlled by the corporation was buying the shares. This type of plan is known as an 'ESOP'. This small difference made this into a Section 14(d) tender offer, which means a third party tender offer, rather than a Section 13(e) tender offer, which applies to corporations buying back their own stock.

The problem was that tender offers under Section 13(e) are handled by a different division of the S.E.C. than those tender offers under Section 14(d). These two different divisions of the S.E.C. had a different interpretation of the same rule.

The rule in question was the 'equal treatment of security

holders' rule. My plan was to pay each stockholder who tendered his shares $1.00 per share plus a bonus of $25 to each stockholder who tendered all of his shares. In other words, a stockholder who tendered his one share would receive $26, whereas a stockholder who tendered his 99 shares would get $124. The $1.00 per share would be paid by the ESOP, whereas the $25 bonus would be paid by the corporation.

I had done many other tender offers in which a bonus exactly like that had been paid. There had never been a problem. However, in this case, the problem arose because a different division of the S.E.C. was handling this particular tender offer. The Division of Corporate Finance, which handles tender offers under Section 14(d), was of the opinion that equal treatment of security holders means that each security holder receives the same amount per share. I disagreed. In other words, they were of the opinion that the payment of the $25 bonus was illegal. However, the other division which handled Section 13(e) tender offers interpreted the same rule as allowing each security holder who tendered all of his shares to receive a special bonus.

In other words, we had two different divisions of the S.E.C. who were interpreting the same S.E.C. rule to mean two different things. I kept calling back and forth to each division and neither one would budge. One point which I always like to make about such situations is that in order to be convicted of a crime or even to be enjoined by a federal district court from violations of the S.E.C. rules, it has to be proven that you 'knowingly' violated the rule. My question is: How can a poor schlunk like me who does not even work for the S.E.C. be expected to know what an S.E.C. rule means when two different divisions of the S.E.C. which played a direct role in the drafting of those rules cannot agree between themselves as to what the rule means?

The end result was that I advised my client that in my opinion the payment of the bonus of $25 was vital to the stated objective of the tender offer, which was to reduce the number of stockholders of record to less than 300 so that the company could de-register under Rule 12g-4. However, I also advised my client that the S.E.C. Division of Corporate Finance felt that the payment of this $25 bonus was illegal. I further advised my client that in my opinion it was extremely unlikely that if we went ahead with this tender offer and paid the $25 bonus, that the S.E.C. would sue to enjoin the offer, for the reason that we had a written opinion from the other division of the S.E.C. which said that the payment of the $25 bonus was legal. In short, I provided my client with all of the facts and left it up to her decision as to whether to pay the $25 bonus and run the gauntlet of possible injunctive action by the S.E.C.

In the end, my client was too chicken to risk a lawsuit from the S.E.C. However, the S.E.C. did agree to start an internal administrative proceeding the two divisions to resolve this difference in interpretation of the S.E.C. rules. This tender offer also had a happy ending. The corporation did manage to reduce its stockholders of record to exactly 299 and therefore was able to de-register under Rule 12g-4.

This episode raises a question which will come up again and again. Every reasonable person agrees that the S.E.C. rules must be followed. However, what if the S.E.C. attorney assigned to supervise your tender offer has an interpretation which you feel is wrong? Of course, the conservative view is to do whatever he says, even if you feel that it is wrong. However, what if the situation is such that if you do what he tells you to do, you will suffer a severe financial loss or the deal will be financially unfeasible or even will collapse altogether?

This is not a hypothetical situation. It happens all the time. The conservative course of action will be simply to abandon the tender offer and forget about it. However, the conservative course of action will never get you the girl. The Mike Tyson approach is more likely to produce results.

Getting back to the $25 bonus, it turned out, as it often will, that the corporation achieved its objective without paying the $25 bonus. However, it could easily have happened differently. Had it paid the $25 bonus, it might have been able to reduce its number of stockholders to 280 or 270 without difficulty. As it was, only by squeezing hard was the number reduced to 299. The sole objective of that company was to reduce its stockholders of record to less than 300 so that it would not have to file 10-K and 10-Q reports any more. Had this objective not been achieved, the offer would have been regarded as a failure.

That case was fairly easy because this was a friendly tender offer. Although the ESOP was a different legal entity, it was controlled by the corporation which was the subject of the tender offer. Nobody was interested in defeating this tender offer. There was only the S.E.C. staff attorney, who was demanding that we pay $25 less to the stockholders than we wanted to pay.

In a hostile tender offer situation, however, you will have an active opponent who will be calling up the S.E.C. complaining daily about every little thing that you are doing. Ultimately, a large percentage of these hostile tender offers wind up in court, when one side sues the other. The S.E.C. is essentially a referee.

What if your opponent violates state corporation laws on a grand scale, but does not violate the disclosure requirements of federal securities laws? Will the S.E.C. sue him to stop him from violating state law? The answer is: Probably not.

Here is one area where your opponent will have an advantage over you. In many areas of securities law regarding tender offers, the law regulates the bidder but does not regulate the target. For example, there is an absolute prohibition under the Williams Act against the party making a tender offer from buying any shares outside of the offer. Therefore, while the offer is pending, you cannot buy shares in the open market. However, your opponent can buy shares. Your opponent can also sell shares. Your opponent can issue new shares. Your opponent can sell a control block to a 'white knight'. Your opponent can declare a special dividend. Your opponent can amend the by-laws. Your opponent can withhold from you its current balance sheet. Your opponent can liquidate the entire corporation. There is nothing under the S.E.C. rules which prevent the target corporation from doing any of these things, even if some of these things happen to violate the state corporation law.

The policy of the S.E.C. is that every hostile tender offer is assigned to one S.E.C. staff attorney. That S.E.C. staff attorney will provide your tender offer with cradle-to-grave service. He will not be the one who will put you in jail, however. That will be handled by the Enforcement Division, which is a different division of the S.E.C. (In reality, the Enforcement Division does not put people in jail. These cases are rare, and are handled by the Department of Justice, not by the S.E.C.)

It is always a mistake to assume that this one S.E.C. staff attorney assigned to monitor your hostile tender offer is acting on his own. You will often find that when you call him he is busy, but that he promptly calls you back on the speaker phone. What is probably going on is that he has got four or five other staff attorneys sitting around the telephone listening to you and taking notes, but only the one attorney does any talking, so you are only aware of him.

He will never reveal this, but when he calls you, he has probably just received a call from the other side complaining about the latest thing which you have done. Again, the S.E.C. is acting essentially as a referee.

Many of the things which the S.E.C. might tell you to do or not to do will seem arbitrary and unreasonable. However, I am forced to concede that in the end their actions have seemed fair and reasonable, once I understood their logic. They have, after all, been through a lot of these tender offers. The attorney assigned to your case might be the attorney who handled in the same fashion the Texaco-Pennzoil case, for example.

Having said that, it will often happen that the S.E.C. attorney calls you up one day and tells you to do one thing, and then calls you up the next day and tells you to do exactly the opposite. This is the reason why you have to have your own copy of the rule book and read it yourself. You might often be in the situation where you have to decide whether to comply with today's demand, at considerable financial expense, or whether to stand your ground and claim that the S.E.C.'s interpretation of the rule is wrong and that yours is right.

Again, this is not a game for children. You can be sure that somebody like T. Boone Pickens did not become famous for doing tender offers by always complying with each and every demand which the S.E.C. ever made of him. However, he also did not get there by flagrantly violating S.E.C. rules. One has to walk a tight-rope, never leaning too far one way or too far to the other.

Justice Rehnquist perhaps put it best when he said that the stock in which I was trading 'has, to put it mildly, a history of sailing close to the wind.' *S.E.C. v. Samuel H. Sloan*, 436 U.S. 103, 109 (1978).

Sailing close to the wind is not necessarily a bad thing. Anyone reading this book has by now realized that tender offers are not for everybody. Anyone filing a hostile tender offer is asking for trouble. Not many people have the stomach for this. It is dangerous business. Yet those who succeed make millions at it.

For example, it is a little known fact that Robert Maxwell was, for most of this career, an obscure publisher of chess books. Chess books? Yes, that is what Maxwell published. It was only during the last few years before his death that he went on a frenzy of tender offers and became one of the giants of the publishing industry. At the time that he died, he was regarded as one of the world's richest men, with assets amounting to billions of dollars. However, only a few weeks later, the truth started to come out. In reality, he was one of the world's most insolvent men, with nearly a billion dollars in negative net worth.

This follows Newton's law of gravity. What goes up, must come down. A few years ago, nobody heard of Maxwell. A few years from now, nobody will remember who he was. There have been so many like him, but their names are all forgotten, except by a few people like me, who study these trends.

There are a few clear S.E.C. rules which you should know. These rules might seem arbitrary, but I can assure you that they are all carved in stone.

1. Thou shalt not buy or sell any securities in the target corporation while the tender offer is pending, except within the context of the tender offer.

2. Any person tendering his shares has the legal right to withdraw his shares up until the final expiration date of the tender offer.

3. Thou shalt not make any pre-payment for the tendered shares. You are not allowed to pay for the shares until after the final expiration date has passed. The reason for this is that the stockholders must have the right to withdraw their shares up until the expiration date. In addition, if you increase the price which you are willing to pay, all stockholders, including those who tendered before you increased the price, must receive the higher amount. If you had already paid for their shares, they will not be able to withdraw them, nor will they be in a position to receive the higher consideration.

Many times, the tender offerer wants to make a tender offer on a first-come-first-served basis. This is highly illegal. For example, suppose you tender for 51% of the shares, with the proviso that the first 51% of all outstanding shares tendered will get paid, and the rest will have their tendered shares returned. For this, you will go to jail.

There is a firm S.E.C. rule that a tender offer must remain open for twenty business days. Business days! This is Rule 14e-1(a). A business day is calculated as follows: You announce your tender offer on Friday, November 1. That is called Day One. Therefore, Monday, November 4 is Day Two. Friday, November 8 is Day Five. Thursday, November 28 would be Day Nineteen, except that this is Thanksgiving Day. Therefore, Friday, November 29 is Day Nineteen and Monday, December 1, is Day Twenty. This comes from Rule 14d-1(b)(6).

Therefore, if your offer commences on Friday, November 1, it should conclude on Monday, December 1.

Be sure to remember Martin Luther King Day and all of the other federal holidays which they keep adding as part of the great communist conspiracy to bring American business to a grinding halt.

The reasoning of the S.E.C. is that if you make an offer on a first-come-first-served-basis, everybody will rush to get in their shares first. If you pay them first, then they will in effect have lost their withdrawal rights. The purpose of the twenty business days rule is to give them ample time to consider your tender offer. If they are forced into a stampede to be the first one to get their shares in, then the purpose of the twenty business days rule will be defeated. Therefore, a person who tenders on the last day must be treated equally with a person who tenders on the first day.

4. Every time a material change occurs, you must notify the stockholders of the material change, and you must extend the offer for an additional ten business days in order to give the stockholders the time to assimilate this new information. You are also not allowed to pay for the shares tendered prior to that extension. You must keep those shares along with the others until the end. This gives the stockholders who have previously tendered their shares the opportunity to withdraw their shares in light of the new information.

Your offer might be extended for another ten days, and then another ten days. Often, these extensions will be forced upon you for reasons beyond your control. You already have 51% and you want to get the thing over with, but the S.E.C. forces you to wait. This often happens.

There might be a bidding war. While dilly-dallying over this, somebody else makes a tender offer for the same target company, but at a higher price. Suddenly, everybody writes you and demands their shares back. You have lost everything, only because of an additional ten business day extension which was forced upon you.

5. Any time a tender offer is extended, you must send a press release by FAX to the Dow Jones News Service, before 9:00 A.M. Eastern Time of the morning after the day on which your tender offer was due to expire. This is required by Rule 14e-1(d)(i). Whether they publish your press release or not is irrelevant. You must send them your press release,

whether they decide to publish it or not.

If your FAX machine is broken, you are just out of luck. Your tender offer is concluded, with no further extensions possible. You had better have a back-up machine available, in case this happens. Your press release must give the date and hour to which the tender offer is extended, plus it must state the approximate number of shares tendered until the present date.

The following are the FAX numbers of organizations to which you might want to send your press release: Dow Jones News Service (212) 416-2658; Investors Business Daily (310) 207-4685; Los Angeles Times (213) 237-4712; Washington Post (202) 334-5564; San Francisco Chronicle (415) 512-8196; Oakland Tribune (510) 645-2771; Financial Information, Inc. (201) 432-9779; Depository Trust Company (212) 709-1093; Shareholder Communications Corporation (212) 809-2656; Securities and Exchange Commission (202) 272-2677 and (202) 272-7050.

6. You are not allowed to make an illusory tender offer. In other words, you must demonstrate a capability of paying for the shares. In addition, you cannot say, 'Tender the shares, and then I will decide whether I will pay for them or not.' However, you may impose conditions. You might say, 'I make a firm contractual commitment to pay for all validly tendered shares, provided only that hell freezes over between now and the expiration date.'

You wait twenty business days. You then go to hell and check out the situation there. If hell has frozen over, you must pay for the tendered shares. However, if hell has not frozen over, then you are prohibited from paying for the tendered shares, without a further ten day extension and notification to the stockholders. You cannot say, 'Hell has not frozen over, but I have decided to pay for the tendered shares anyway.'

Instead, what you must do is you must write another letter to the stockholders. That letter will say: 'Contrary to expectations, hell has not frozen over. However, I am still interested in buying the shares. Therefore, I am withdrawing the condition that hell must freeze over. Instead, I am imposing the following new conditions. I am also extending the offer for an additional ten business days in order to give the stockholders time to evaluate these new conditions in the light of recent developments. If, after ten business days, those conditions are met, I will pay for the tendered shares. If those conditions are not met, I may make a further extension or I may withdraw the offer, but I may not conclude the offer without a further ten day extension.'

Chapter Eighteen

Defensive Measures

Today, we are at an all time low point in the level of corporate accountability. Corporate executives are doing things today which nobody would have dreamed of a few years ago. Multi-million dollar annual salaries are being taken by executives of corporations whose profits are actually declining. A corporation's management will announce lay-offs of several thousand assembly line workers, while at the same time voting themselves a hefty raise.

Many top corporate executives and directors cannot even justify their position. Their stock holdings in their corporation are miniscule. Their experience in the industry is limited. They first became a director because they guaranteed a safe vote to a friend of a friend.

This situation, which is really a serious problem for America, provides a ready answer to the often raised problem of 'Japan bashing'. Americans and American politicians are concerned only about an increasing number of Americans who are losing their jobs. Americans have no great love for the chairmen of those corporations who are tightening everybody's belt except for their own. If those people who are drawing multi-million dollar salaries while everybody else is suffering got thrown out on the street, everybody would applaud. Nobody would really object to a take-over by new Japanese owners, provided only that the average rank and file worker does not lose his job.

However, the American tendency towards corporate greed will cause problems for you in your tender offer. It is a discouraging fact that many corporate executives would prefer to destroy their own corporation rather than to allow somebody else to take it over.

One of the reasons why it was earlier stated that at the outset you should try to buy 4.999% of the total outstanding shares is that this gives you some cushion. It requires you to spend some money. However, it gives you some standing in the likely event that this matter arrives in federal district court. For example, under California law, a holder of 5% of the stock in a corporation can call for a new election of directors upon ten days notice. You might want to do this while the tender offer is going on. Other states have similar laws. You need to be familiar with the statutory law and the case law of the state of incorporation prior to undertaking a tender offer.

A useful case to read on the subject of tender offers is *Stahl v. Apple Bancorp, Inc.*, 579 Atlantic Reporter 1115 (Delaware 1990). There, the owner of 30% of the stock who had made a tender offer for the remaining outstanding shares was unable to compel a special stockholder's election.

A good second case to read is *In Re Anderson, Clayton Stockholders Litigation*, 519 Atlantic Reporter 2d 669 and 680 (Delaware 1986). There are actually about five lengthy reported decisions regarding this tender offer. The judge seems to have been both fair and knowledgeable, which is more than can be said for many judges. I will not attempt to explain that case or its outcome, since that would require the one hundred pages which the decisions themselves take. If you seriously want to undertake a tender offer, have your storefront lawyer obtain a photocopy from the local law library.

It is noteworthy that both of the above cases were tried in the Delaware Chancery Court, not in the federal court. Incidentally, both cases had the same judge, whose name was Allen. Remember that the federal law deals almost entirely with disclosure. If you want to demand a new stockholder election after you have acquired a majority of the outstanding shares or if you want to enjoin the sale the 'crown jewels' among the corporate assets, your case should properly be filed in state court, not in federal court. However, lawyers are sometimes reluctant to file such cases in state court. They complain of weak minded state court judges. This complaint does not apply to Delaware however, because the judges there know far more about this than does the average federal district court judge.

Here is a good example of why you should fear your own lawyer's advice. When he tells you to file a case in federal court, bear in mind that he will charge you a much higher fee to fight the case in federal court than to fight the same case in state court.

One reason why you want to buy at least 4.999% of the total outstanding shares prior to making a tender offer is that the offer itself will cause the stock to go up. You will therefore have an instant profit. Don't try selling your stock on the open market while the tender offer is pending, however. That would be illegal. Also, don't tell your friends to sell. That is even more illegal and might result in actual jail time.

What will the target corporation do? The answer is: Almost anything is possible. Before undertaking this tender offer, you should have done a psychoanalysis of the all of the board members of the target corporation. If the broad consists of the president, his wife, and his three children, you might have a tough time. If the board consists of high profile people like Gerald Ford, whoever he is, you will find that they have no real interest in fighting a knock down and drag out battle. They will bail out quickly just to avoid damage to their reputations. They will allow you to take over the corporation without difficulty.

The main point is that you have to assume the worst and be prepared for that. However, even if the board of the target corporation decides strenuously to oppose you, they will be reluctant to do so in such a way that clearly harms the stockholders. They might declare a special dividend for example, ridding the company of excess cash. If you already own 4.999% of the total outstanding shares, some of that money will come to you. Indeed, anything they do will be likely to make the stock price go higher, which benefits you as one of the major stockholders.

Remember, though, that if the tender offer collapses, the stock price will probably fall lower than it was before the tender offer was announced.

One reason why it has been stressed repeatedly that the corporation you intend to take over must have solid assets with solid values is that if the corporation is sound financially, it becomes more difficult for the management to pull off some flim-flam which will defeat your tender offer and which also does not benefit you in some way. On the other hand, if the stock is a high flier with no real assets, damage to the reputation of the corporation alone can make its shares worthless.

It might happen that the management of the target corporation decides to give in and allow you to take them over. The chances of this happening greatly increase if you allow them to vote themselves golden parachutes, permitting them to stuff some money into their pockets before vacating the corporate premises. You may not be happy about this, but it has been allowed by the Delaware courts.

If they agree to allow you to take over, you probably will not want to go through a new election of directors, because that will be a long procedure requiring the filing of a proxy statement with the S.E.C. and a wait of at least 30 days. You will want to be sitting in the President's chair today.

In that case, one way to achieve this purpose will be through the by-laws of the target corporation. Usually, the by-laws contain a provision that if a vacancy develops on the board of directors, the remaining directors can elect a new board member.

Therefore, what you do is that all but one of the members of the existing board resign. After that, the one remaining board member appoints you and several of your colleagues to fill the vacant seats on the board. After that, the one remaining member of the old board resigns. You then fill the one remaining seat with a person selected by you.

What happens if the old board decides not to cooperate?

There are many answers to this. Under the law of Delaware and other states, there is a statutory provision which allows the majority stockholder in a corporation to remove the entire existing board of a corporation and to appoint his own new board. In California, this provision is found under Section 303 of the California Corporation Code. Other states have similar provisions.

According to law textbooks, this problem should not arise. The law books say that once an outside group acquires 51% of the stock, the directors are all supposed to resign. The theory is that no director will risk a lawsuit by attempting to serve against the wishes of a majority of the stockholders.

What if the directors refuse to vacate? This occurrence is extremely rare, but it has happened to me. The answer is supposed to be to apply to the courts for relief.

Almost all of the case law in this field has been decided in the Delaware courts. A tiny state like California, for example, will not have much law, because few major corporations are incorporated in California because of the restrictive blue sky laws there. Since California has almost no case law of its own, it will tend to follow Delaware law.

What if all the directors resign, but, out of spite, they refuse first to appoint you to replace them?

This raises a tough question.

If there is no board at all because all of the directors have resigned, you have the right under state corporation law to appoint a new board by written consent of the majority of stockholders. However, there is a problem with this. Under S.E.C. Rule 14c-2, twenty days prior to the election of directors by written consent, you must distribute an information statement, on a similar form as a proxy statement, to the security holders. Moreover, under S.E.C. Rule 14c-5, you must file five copies of a preliminary copy of that information statement 10 days prior to mailing that statement to the security holders.

In other words, this rule appears to require you to wait for a total of a minimum of 30 days between the time that you acquire a majority of the outstanding shares to the time that you can take working control of the subject corporation. However, state corporation law allows you to take control immediately. Again, we have the problem of 'conflict of laws.'

This is a matter of critical importance. Remember that during the intervening 30 days, the old corporate president will still be there, stuffing as much cash into his pockets as possible. He will be burning and otherwise destroying the old corporate files. He will be writing all kinds of checks to his friends and so on.

My opinion is that this 30 day waiting period does not apply in this situation. During the course of your tender offer, you have conducted numerous mailings to the stockholders. The stockholders know that your intention from the beginning has been to throw the old management out on the street. They tendered their shares to you in full knowledge of this fact. It seems illogical that you should, after all this, be required to wait an additional thirty days to accomplish your purpose.

Fortunately, this particular situation is rare. I know of only one instance where such an extreme thing has happened. Unfortunately, in that one case, it happened to me.

Chapter Nineteen

A Case History

Every tender offer is different. Reciting a bunch of examples of tender offers in the past and what the outcome was in each case might make interesting reading, but is unlikely to be of much practical use to a party seriously intending to make a tender offer. For that reason, I will just give one actual example of what can happen. I feel that this example is particularly instructive.

Hardcourt Brace Jovanovich, Inc. was, and indeed still is, one of the largest book publishers in the world. In 1987, an unknown group, presumably controlled by Robert Maxwell, expressed an interest in purchasing the then cash rich corporation for $44 per share. The reaction by management was to recapitalize the corporation in such a way that nobody would ever want to buy it. They spun off the cash, and then issued junk bonds to saddle the corporation with enormous debt, debt which could never be repaid.

This recapitalization had its intended effect. Maxwell immediately lost interest and forgot about the whole thing, assuming that he was ever seriously interested at all. The problem was that Hardcourt Brace was no longer really a viable concern and, in 1991, had a brush with bankruptcy.

The following details are provided by a recent proxy statement issued by Hardcourt Brace:

'On May 18, 1987, Hardcourt Brace received a letter from

The British Printing & Communication Corporation plc ('BPCC') that proposed a discussion be held concerning BPCC's acquisition of Hardcourt, Brace at $44 per share in cash for all of the outstanding shares. The letter stated, among other things, that BPCC was prepared to meet as promptly as possible to review all aspects of such a transaction, including price. It also stated that, based upon discussions with its financial advisors, BPCC had reason to believe that the financing for such a transaction is available. During the period May 21 through May 26, 1987, the Board of Directors of Hardcourt Brace held five meetings to consider the BPCC proposal and other possible alternatives.

On May 26, 1987, the Board of Directors voted (by unanimous consent of those present) to reject the BPCC Proposal. In so doing, the Board considered a number of factors, including the business prospects of the company and the value of its various businesses as compared in price to the BPCC Proposal, which price was 11.4 percent over the highest trading price of the Company's shares from January through May 15, 1987, the last trading day before the BPCC Proposal. The Board also took into account (i) then current multiples paid for book publishing companies (ii) the written opinion of First Boston, the Company's financial adviser at the time, (iii) the fact that the BPCC Proposal did not include firm financing, (iv) concern as to the effect of an acquisition of the Company by BPCC on the Company's employees and customers, and (v) uncertainty as to the identity of the persons or entities owning or controlling Pergamon Holding Foundation, a Liechtenstein trust that BPCC had indicated was the majority shareholder of BPCC.

On May 26, 1987, the Board of Directors also voted to approve a recapitalization plan. In adopting the recapitalization plan, the Board consulted with its legal and financial advisers as well as with the Company's senior management.

Under the recapitalization, on July 27, 1987, the Company paid a special dividend to its common shareholders of $40 in cash and one share of preferred stock. The Special Dividend aggregated approximately $1.6 billion in cash and approximately 40.5 million shares of Preferred stock having an aggregate liquidation preference of approximately $546.7 Million. In order to finance the recapitalization, the Company (i) entered into a credit agreement which provided for a working capital facility which permits borrowings of up to $350 million, (ii) sold a total of 4.8 million shares of common stock to the Hardcourt Brace Employee Stock Ownership Plan for $49.3 million ($10.25 per share), (iii) subsequently sold an additional 10 million shares to to the ESOP for approximately $99 million ($9.88 per share) (iv) sold in an underwritten public offering three issues of subordinated discount debentures in an aggregate principal amount of $1.247 billion, and used the net proceeds of approximately $965 million to repay indebtedness incurred in connection with the recapitalization.

In considering the recapitalization, the company considered that after giving effect to the recapitalization the company would become highly leveraged and certain factors, including the substantial indebtedness to be incurred in the recapitalization, would increase the risk associated with and could otherwise adversely affect the value of an investment in the company. It was also expected that the declaration of the special dividend associated with the recapitalization would result in a substantial negative balance in shareholders equity and a significant decrease in net earnings or increase in net losses would result from the substantial increase in interest expense associated with the higher levels of debt required to effect the recapitalization. The significantly higher ratio of debt to equity would, among other things, affect the Company's planned capital expenditures, its ability to make future acquisitions and its ability to pay future cash dividends. The company anticipated that it would not be able to pay any dividends on any class of its capital stock for at least five years.'

The last paragraph above should be read carefully. What it actually states is that the recapitalization was done in such a way as would increase the risk associated with the value of an investment in the company and would result in a substantial negative balance in shareholders equity and a significant decrease in net earnings or increase in net losses.

Stated differently, the Hardcourt Brace management decided to destroy the earnings potential of the corporation just to prevent Maxwell from taking over. However, the stockholders were not directly hurt. The stockholders received $40 per share in cash, plus one share of preferred, plus they still continued to hold the common shares which were apparently worth nearly $10 per share. In short, the stockholders got more than they probably would have received had Maxwell been allowed to take over.

On the other hand, three types of junk bonds were issued. The purchasers of those junk bonds eventually lost money. Later on, the purchasers of the subordinated discount bonds were paid off at the rate of only 40.975 cents on the dollar. However, one needs not to feel sorry for them. Anybody purchasing an issue of junk bonds can justifiably expect to receive what he paid for.

The employees may have lost money. The company issued 14.8 million new shares and sold them at an average of about $10 per share to a captive investor, the Employee Stock Ownership Plan.

Perhaps the biggest looser was the American economy. In this case, the company survived, in weaker condition, but only because it was eventually taken over by General Cinema Corporation in 1991.

There are many lessons to be learned from this case: some good, some bad. It is noteworthy that the ownership of BPCC was never revealed. Is was only assumed that Maxwell was the owner. In addition, no tender offer was ever filed. Hardcourt Brace took the precipitous action they did only because of being threatened by BPCC. Maxwell is now dead, and nobody will ever know whether he was bluffing or not.

BPCC was a Liechtenstein corporation. Liechtenstein is a tiny postage-stamp country located next to Switzerland which has a unique system of allowing corporations to be formed where it is impossible to find out the true owner. It is doubtful whether the S.E.C. would allow a tender offer to be filed by a Liechtenstein corporation unless that corporation was prepared to disclose its true owner. However, that situation never came up, because Maxwell never filed the tender offer.

The way that a Liechtenstein corporation works is roughly as follows: The corporation is formed in Liechtenstein by a Liechtenstein lawyer, who must be a native born citizen of

Liechtenstein. The lawyer becomes the nominal owner. Only the lawyer knows the name of the real owner. Nothing is filed. However, the lawyer irrevocably assigns his ownership rights to the real owner. With this document, the real owner then goes to neighboring Switzerland and establishes a bank account in the name of the corporation. The Swiss bank knows the law of Liechtenstein. It knows that the Liechtenstein lawyer is not the real owner and that the person to whom the ownership rights were assigned is the real owner. It opens the bank account with the real owner having sole signing power and the Liechtenstein lawyer having no right to know the whereabouts of the bank account. Even if the Liechtenstein lawyer comes to the bank and proves that he is the owner on paper, the Swiss bank will not reveal any information to him about the bank account, nor will it allow him to withdraw any money from the bank account. Finally, and most importantly, if the Liechtenstein lawyer is ever subpoenaed before any court of competent jurisdiction anywhere in the world and is ordered to testify and to reveal to the court who the true owners are, and if he does comply and if he does reveal the true owners, he will then be sentenced to a long prison term for this, if and when he ever goes back to his native Liechtenstein.

Understandably, the S.E.C. looks at such arrangements with a jaundiced eye. It is doubtful whether Maxwell or anyone else would ever be allowed to take over an American public company through the medium of a Liechtenstein corporation. However, Maxwell accomplished his purpose. He terrorized the largest publishing company in the world into self-destructing, just by threatening to try to take them over.

Chapter Twenty

A Second Example

To avoid leading the reader down the primrose path into believing that all of this is easy, I want to provide an unfortunate example of what can happen.

Many readers may have heard the name of James T. Sherwin. He happens to be a person whom I know well, because I played my first chess game against him in 1960 in St. Louis (he won) and have played many chess games against him since then. He is an International Chess Master and, in 1957 and 1958, he was the number three officially ranked chess player in the United States, behind only Bobby Fischer and Samuel Reshevsky.

However, now, he is not even ranked in the top 100 in chess. The reason: He essentially gave up serious chess to become one of America's top corporate lawyers.

It is rare for any man to reach the top in two fields. However, virtually every lawyer in America has heard of James Sherwin, but they do not know that he is a chess player. At the same time, every chess player in the world has heard of James Sherwin, but they do not know that he is a lawyer.

I, myself, did not realize how important Sherwin was in the field of law until 1982, when I mentioned to a big Madison Avenue lawyer that I knew Sherwin, and he offered to pay me a considerable amount of money just to arrange a personal introduction. I told him that I did not want his money. I then took him down to the Manhattan Chess Club and allowed him to watch me play a game of five-minute chess against Sherwin. (I lost again.)

Unfortunately, thereafter, Sherwin went from the top to the bottom in the field of law. The reader might find what happened to him to be instructive.

Among his other duties, Sherwin was on the board of directors of GAF Corporation, one of the largest corporations in America. Jefferies & Co. in Los Angeles, a securities dealer, was trading heavily in the stock of GAF. This was going on during the period when everybody was making tender offers to take over everybody else.

At some point, Sherwin said to Jefferies, 'If you buy the stock of GAF Corporation, and if you lose money, I will make it up to you.' Jefferies thereafter bought the stock. The stock went down. Jefferies lost $40,000. Jefferies called Sherwin and asked for the $40,000.

At this point, Sherwin told his secretary to cut a check for $40,000. The check was prepared for his signature. Then Sherwin thought better of it. He decided that the payment of this $40,000 might be illegal.

This was clearly not a problem of money. GAF is a billion dollar corporation. The sum of $40,000 is meaningless to a corporation like that.

However, the check itself was of great significance. This check, made out but never signed, was later used to convict Sherwin.

What happened is that at a later date, Jefferies was indicted for stock fraud for reasons which had nothing to do with Sherwin or with GAF. The prosecutors offered Jefferies a deal. They would give him a lenient sentence if he would name names and become a professional witness, testifying against everyone whom he believed might be guilty of something.

This happens to be a dangerous procedure. In many cases, when an individual enters into the Professional Witness Protection Program established under the auspices of the United States Department of Justice, he simply testifies against anybody whom he happens to have a grudge against. The professional witness does not testify against his friends. He does not testify against those persons whom he believes that he will do business with in the future. Rather, he testifies against those who were already his enemies to begin with.

Jefferies had a grudge against Sherwin because he felt that Sherwin had stiffed him for the $40,000. This was a big amount for Jefferies, even though it was a small amount for Sherwin.

Therefore, Jefferies used his newly acquired status as a professional witness to testify against Sherwin. Sherwin was indicted. This indictment against a director of one of the largest corporations in the world made the front page of the New York Times and almost every other newspaper. Eventually, Sherwin was convicted. The case is still probably pending on appeal.

Now, the key question is: What did Sherwin do wrong?

Actually, the astute reader of this book will have already figured out what Sherwin did wrong. It is to be recalled that several times in this book I have warned against forming any sort of group or combination in connection with a tender offer, unless that group or combination is disclosed to the

S.E.C. Perhaps you were not paying much attention, but I had a reason for saying that.

When Sherwin said to Jefferies, 'If you buy the stock of GAF Corporation, and if you lose money, I will make it up to you,' he thereby formed a group or combination in clear violation of the statutory language of the Securities Exchange Act of 1934 and the rules and regulations promulgated thereunder and thereby engaged in a manipulative, deceptive and fraudulent practice in connection with a scheme or artifice to defraud for the clear purpose of controlling the price above the level which would otherwise have been dictated by the normal forces of the law of supply and demand.

Is that clear enough?

A few years later, I was sitting in a chess club in Kuala Lumpur, Malaysia, talking to Anand, an Indian child prodigy who is now officially ranked as the number five chess player in the world. I happened to mention to Anand the moves of a chess game that Sherwin had once played against Petrosian. 'Sherwin?', Anand said, 'Isn't he that guy who swindled that old lady in Los Angeles out of her entire life savings?'

This is very upsetting. Here is Anand, a Tamil Tiger from Madras, India, who knows a lot about chess but probably knows little if anything about the stock market but who has heard the news and believes that Jefferies, a convicted stock manipulator, is instead an old lady in Los Angeles.

The irony of this is that there is probably no person more fastidious about following the law than Sherwin. A lesser person would simply have denied the entire conversation with Jefferies and gotten off. Sherwin got to the top in the field of corporate law by being an expert in a complex field of law and by following the law exactly. However, he was a real man operating in a real world. He made a careless remark in a conversation with his stock broker. Later on, it occurred to him that there might be something improper about this, and for that reason decided not to mail the check for $40,000.

This, indeed, is the reason that he was convicted. Being a top corporate lawyer in this particular field of law, the prosecution argued that Sherwin, unlike any normal person, could not contend that he did not know what the law was.

Almost anybody else but Sherwin would have denied the entire conversation or would have mailed the check for $40,000 or would have done any one of a number of other things which would have gotten him off the hook. Instead, he was prosecuted. It was also a stroke of exceptionally bad luck that his stock broker later on changed jobs and became a professional witness. Even if Sherwin ultimately gets off and does not have to serve time in jail, he and his corporation will still have paid more than one million dollars in legal fees to defend this case. Needless to say, he has also lost his job and is no longer with GAF Corp. He also had to resign as Chairman of the American Chess Foundation.

Any one reading this will be thinking about the many times when his own stock broker has said to him, 'If you buy this stock, I guarantee you that it will not go down,' or else, 'If you lose money on this stock, I will make it up to you.' Brokers make this sort of statement all the time. When a broker does it, he is in clear violation of the rules of the New York Stock Exchange.

Sherwin, however, was not a stock broker. Sherwin was a private citizen. Jefferies was a stock broker. It seems strange that Sherwin was prosecuted for this unfortunate remark, whereas Jefferies was never prosecuted.

The truth of the matter is that it is strictly random who gets prosecuted and who does not. What makes the Sherwin case remarkable is that he was punished so severely and sentenced to jail for such a minor every day infraction which almost every stock broker has engaged in at some time or another in his career.

Another point of note is that it is to be recalled that in Japan, the unwritten rule among the so-called 'stable shareholders' is that 'I'll buy your stock, and you'll buy mine.'

What the Sherwin case shows is that the standard securities practice in Japan would be entirely illegal in America. Stated differently, if the U.S. securities laws were imposed upon Japan, then every corporate portfolio manager in Japan would already be in jail.

Chapter Twenty One

Summary and Conclusion

While writing this book, I have avoided advocating any specific plan or system for doing tender offers. Rather, I have attempted to provide the basic information one needs to know.

I have been reluctant to go further than that because every deal is different. Also, I might inadvertently advocate something which is considered improper. Also, I am fearful that so many people might follow my suggestions as to establish a certain type of tender offer.

I would like to point out, however, that there are certain things which one sees again and again when reading through tender offer documents filed with the S.E.C. One is that the actual bidder making a tender offer is usually a freshly formed corporation with no assets.

It will be recalled that there is one chapter in this book on how to form a corporation. The reason for this is that the bidder will often find it useful to form a corporation solely for the purpose of acting as the nominal bidder in a tender offer. However, in that case, the balance sheet of the parent company must be disclosed.

In the case of a Japanese company attempting to take over an American company, it would probably be a good idea for many reasons, including Japanese tax and American tax reasons, to form a fresh corporation in Delaware which does nothing else but bid for the shares of the target corporation.

Regarding financing, the bidder can legally avoid disclosing his own financial position by obtaining from a bank a firm loan guarantee to pay for all shares validly tendered. The loan guarantee would presumably be secured by the true bidder's assets. However, the management of the target corporation would have no way of knowing the whereabouts of the assets of the bidder. This would work only if the tender offer was entirely for cash, and not in exchange for other securities.

I do not want to advocate this course of action. I merely want to point out this possibility.

One thing which should never be done is to put the assets of the bidder into escrow. In the case of a successful tender offer, the majority of all shares tendered will probably be tendered through Depository Trust Company at 7 Hanover Square in New York City. Therefore, the money to pay for the tendered shares should be sent directly from the bidder to DTC, without using any intermediaries. Otherwise, remember the old saying, 'Tis many a slip, twixt the cup and the lip.'

Although a tender offer might be completed through the use of junk bonds, I have not discussed this possibility much because I do not want to appear to be advocating it. In addition, the S.E.C. rules have changed and will continue to change in this field. I might inadvertently wind up advocating a course of action which has been declared to be illegal by some obscure S.E.C. interpretative letter of which I am not aware. Also, junk bonds are no longer fashionable these days.

The Slave Children of Thomas Jefferson

by Samuel H. Sloan

What do the retired Chairman of the Board of DuPont Chemical Corporation, the first black Assemblyman in the history of the State of California, one on the co-founders of the NAACP, the first black tenured faculty member of any college in America, the first black woman ever to graduate from Vassar College, and a judge recently appointed by President George Bush, all have in common?

All of them are direct descendants of the slave children of Thomas Jefferson.

Many people have heard the story that President Thomas Jefferson, the author of the Declaration of Independence and one of the Founding Fathers of the United States of America, produced children from his slaves.

Is this story really true, and what happened to those children? Is Govenor Douglas Wilder of Virginia one of those descendants? These questions as well as many others are answered in *The Slave Children of Thomas Jefferson*.